Andrea is divorced with two grown-up children. She now lives in Hammamet with her Tunisian fiancé. Andrea is an English language teacher for foreign students and has worked in the UK and Spain. She currently lives in Tunisia and is now concentrating on her poetry and the sequel to *Only a Yorkshire Lass*!

To the Bataillard family
who gave me back my sanity.

With grateful thanks to Fernando and Fran
for their infinite patience and help with typing.

Andrea Dridi

ONLY A YORKSHIRE LASS

AUSTIN MACAULEY PUBLISHERS™

LONDON • CAMBRIDGE • NEW YORK • SHARJAH

A CIP catalogue record for this title is available from the British Library.

ISBN 9781528987660 (Paperback)
ISBN 9781528987691 (ePub e-book)

www.austinmacauley.com

First Published (2021)
Austin Macauley Publishers Ltd
25 Canada Square
Canary Wharf
London
E14 5LQ

Table of Contents

Introduction

I've actually started writing my autobiography so many times. Even got as far as three pages. But what the hell, who wants to read a book about me?

I'm not famous, I'm not even infamous. Just an ordinary, ageing, overweight, arthritic, not pretty woman, born in a town 58 years ago that many people outside South Yorkshire haven't even heard of.

But sifting through photo albums, souvenirs and some long-forgotten memories, I realise that I have had a very interesting, colourful, strange and even at times, an enviable life.

Human life has many phases, not unlike that of the animal kingdom. I certainly was an ugly pupa; pity I didn't make it to the beautiful butterfly stage. The ugly duckling that didn't turn into a swan. Luckily for me, that attribute, having skipped me, re-emerged, from my parents, in my children and my beautiful granddaughter.

But more of them later, much, much later.

I have battled with drink problems, gambling problems, not to mention weight issues and from the age of 15, have suffered severe mental health problems. All of which contributed to the breakdown of my 30 marriage and my being sectioned for three months after a complete nervous breakdown.

I have experienced abortions, miscarriages, attempted suicides, lesbian relationships, a sexual attack at the age of 11, which no amount of years can erase, never to be spoken of to parents or grownups at the time, and raped whilst under the influence of alcohol. A torrid love affair with a man young enough to be my son. I have lived in virtual poverty and the life of a millionaire. I have met and known a US president and UK prime minister, royalty, peers of the realm, MPs, rock stars and famous people from all walks of life, all of which have enriched or shaped the journey to where I am now.

Writing my story has had its high and low points. It fills me with sadness, regret, joy, happiness, amazement and longing for the past and fear for the future. All the emotions which contribute to the rich pattern of life—my life!

It's an evening in April 2009, and I am sitting here alone, as usual, music playing. A half bottle of cheap white wine and an assortment of prescribed drugs staring back at me from the table as I struggle to focus having left a letter for my son. How did I ever get to this point?

Chapter 1
Early Years

I was born in the early spring of 1951 the first child of George and Shirley, who had only been married since July 1950. As you can imagine 58 years ago, the wedding was a foregone conclusion.

I spent the first six months of my life at the home of my paternal grandmother and was christened at the church where my parents had met at the youth club of the church. After which my parents and I moved a short distance away into a rented property which was owned by my maternal grandfather. Some eight months later, my second sibling was born and 22 months later, my mother produced yet another daughter.

Although my father was happy with three daughters, he did hanker after a boy and fostered a small boy of whom I have only vague recollections and for some reason or another, it didn't work out. Four years after my second sibling was born, my parents produced yet another daughter!

My childhood until the age of eight was a relatively happy one although it was punctuated by unwarranted bouts of physical punishment by my mother. "Spare the rod and spoil the child" was the by-gone motto.

There was always the issue of mealtimes. If anything was left on your plate, it was put in the pantry until the next mealtime when it was brought out again and unless it was eaten first, nothing fresh would be allowed to pass your lips. Perhaps it was a throwback from the days of rationing. Who knows? Sweet rationing was still in force at that time.

I now know, and realise, that these outbursts of my mother's were borne out of sheer frustration with, and resentment of, her lot in life at that time. She was virtually housebound with four children under the age of seven by the time she was 26 and a husband at work all day.

I also feel that having married because of me, the brunt of her anger fell on me.

Our home was a "passage" house in the middle of a long row of terraced property. There was no bathroom, just a tin bath in front of the fire at weekends, with multiple users and an outside toilet with neatly cut up newspapers—no Andrex then! Although we did progress to Izal which was only marginally softer on the bum! The small kitchen housed a copper boiler and washboard with which to service a family of six's weekly laundry. Mondays will always remind me of washdays—the smell of soapy water and a steam-filled kitchen. And of course, the smell of stew—an easy meal to prepare on such a busy day.

The terrace was like a little community in itself and everyone knew everyone, and I suspect everyone's business too. But having said that, there was no shortage of help if anyone was in need of it, post wartime camaraderie I suspect.

I knew everyone in our "yard". The Morgan family at the other end and then Grannie Morgan next door to them. Then here were the Chesters. It was their garden our rabbit would liberate itself to in order to mutilate Mr Chester's vegetable patch.

The Smiths were in between them and us and were very helpful to my mother.

Across the passage in the next yard was Miss Taylor, a spinster and Mr and Mrs Hudson, he was a dustbin man (I can't remember the politically correct term nowadays) and he had some wonderful "finds" which he always shared out among the community.

I do have some happy memories from that house when my father was alive. I remember having piano lessons, making myself giddy on a red and yellow mobo roundabout in the front room, and I remember quite vividly my seventh birthday party, my only one I believe, when I won a charm bracelet at "pass the parcel". There was the incredibly bad winter when my father took us to school on the sledge wearing a pair of galoshes which you don't see now just jazzy wellington boots. For some bizarre reason I also remember that all chairs and sofas had 'chair back' covers as the young men including my father always wore brylcreem (today's equivalent of gel) and it was a nuisance to clean off!

I remember, too, my sister being knocked down by a bicycle, crossing the road to see our great grandmother and having to have stitches in her forehead. Our great grandparents lived across the road almost exactly opposite to our house. There were always sweets or biscuits when we visited. In those days, every home seemed to have a biscuit tin and some sort of receptacle for sweets. My great grandfather was often to be found sitting on the wall of the front garden, smoking his pipe and watching the world go by. That was the time when neighbours knew each other and not a day went by without having a conversation with someone in the street.

I also feel that it was an incredibly safe era in society. We were allowed to go across the road alone to the fields and down to the River Don and watch the loch keeper open and close the gates. We would often stand on the pedestrian bridge to watch the trains go by too. Small things were amusing and exciting then, and of course free. How times have changed. Perhaps the word "paedophile" hadn't been invented then?

Another memory I have is of having appendicitis and being taken to the hospital by ambulance. My mother told me later that they had forgotten to obtain parents' signature for the operation and had to come back to the house dressed in theatre gowns. Or so she says!

Because it was Christmas, the hospital tried to send as many children home as possible and I was sent home on Christmas Eve with my stitches in a box wrapped in cotton wool, which I kept for several months before they disintegrated. That Christmas, I received a beautiful wooden desk of which I was very fond of.

There was a cellar in our house for keeping coal. Nearly every household used coal in those days, and the pits were thriving. Living in Rotherham, most boys expected to end up in the pits like their fathers and grandfathers before them. Or in the vast steel works immortalised in that classic film *The Full Monty* (after they closed down!).

The cellar was a familiar hideout for my mother whenever there was a storm. She was terrified of thunder and, in particular, lightning and would gather us together there if my father was out for the duration of the storm.

As parents pass on their genes to their children, likewise phobias and fears are transmitted and I still retain a fear of storms to this day, along with my dread of dogs, which was another of my mother's inexplicable fears. But the greatest of all my fears was, and still is to some extent, dread of the dark and night. I can only attribute this to the fact that when my father was out playing billiards, my mother would wake me up, dress my sleep craving, shivering body and send me down the dark passage to the fish and chip shop!

I loved, adored and respected my father greatly and he, in return, spent the majority of his free time with his children but me in particular as the eldest. I was a good student and he was an even better teacher. On our walks to the sarsaparilla shop, he would teach me to recite numbers in French or do mental arithmetic.

He was also possessed with a great sense of humour which on occasions backfired. We had a pet rabbit called Sandy McCab of all things and one meal time when we were actually eating rabbit stew, which was very popular at that time and perhaps cheap, my father said that it was Sandy as he had got out of his hutch and eaten some of the vegetables in our neighbour's garden. There were floods of tears until we were convinced by a trip to the hutch that our beloved pet was still in it. My father had passed for, and attended, Rotherham Grammar School for boys and then obtained a scholarship to Sheffield University which was some feat in 1946, belonging to a one-parent family. My father began work after his national service as a student teacher but at that time, the pay was too poor to sustain his growing family and he began work as a metallurgist at Arthur Lee & Sons—a career at which he excelled given his mathematical ability and curious mind.

His talents didn't end there. He was an accomplished sportsman and even had the opportunity to play at "Lords". (He was known as Tiger Norton to his fans—an incredible fast bowler.) He listed among his acquaintances the great Fred Trueman and I often would accompany him to matches. He was also an ardent football supporter and I remember vividly being seated on his shoulders at football matches when there were actually crowds attending the "Millers" matches (RUFC). He was also a keen rugby player which unfortunately led to him acquiring a broken jaw on one occasion.

My father's frustration at my mother's dissatisfaction with her lot, pressure of work and financial constraints took its toll on him and he would often explode. I remember him breaking a chair and a mirror, but his frustrations were never taken out on the family physically. However, my mother's frustrations always seemed to be taken out on me even at the young age of three or four years old.

She was often upstairs and if there was any noise or a problem downstairs, she would call down for me to fetch up the hairbrush. It had a very hard back to it. She would then proceed to whack me on the back of my legs and then order me to take the brush back downstairs!

After months, although I suspect, years of nagging, my mother persuaded my father to move to a new council estate at K.Park. The attraction was the modern bathroom and inside toilet even though the property was miles from our extended family and meant my father had to commute much further to work.

The house was bigger than our old one but I had to share a bed with one of my sisters when I had previously had a cosy room of my own.

We had so many nearby places to explore along with numerous newfound friends, most of whom my father disapproved of. Greasbrough Dam was a favourite because of the water lilies and all the pond life there. Also the walk there, particularly in spring or summer, meant that we could collect armfuls of beautiful wild flowers and bring home jam jars full of tadpoles and pondweed. Once, we even managed to trap a water lily but only at the expense of ruining a pair of shoes and socks!

We were all fish out of water but my father in particular. We were deemed to be "posh" by the way we spoke and "stuck-up" because of our thirst for education and knowledge, something which has never left me.

My father disapproved of us climbing trees, running up and down the street and shouting with our neighbour's children. He was a stickler for correct forms of speech and was very unhappy about some of the newfound phrases particularly "ever so" instead of "very".

Sometimes he would have outbursts of temper which although they didn't last very long were extremely frightening. One particular evening when my mother was out with a neighbour, my younger siblings were in bed and I wanted to watch TV a little longer. My father said that it was too late and when I started to cry, he shouted, 'Blood and sand,' his way of swearing and banged the table behind me where he was doing some work. Needless to say, I stayed up a little longer and my father was his normal self again within a matter of minutes.

My father never felt part of the community and he never settled there. There was tension between my parents; even a child could sense it. And as I learned later, my father was under pressure at work due to his honesty and integrity.

The one person he did discuss it with was his older brother, my uncle Herbert. Uncle Herbert had 4 daughters too and a 2-family outing would entail 4 adults and 8 children squeezing into my uncle's large black humber car. My father and my uncle had agreed to meet two weeks after they had spoken on the telephone but by then, my father had already taken his own life.

My father had begun taking driving lessons and was intending to buy a small car to enable the family to become more mobile. He had also recently obtained a passport as he was to travel to Geneva on business. My parents had also made the decision to move from our short-lived home. The future looked altogether brighter until that fateful day in July 1959.

My mother was sitting on a chair in the living room. She was crying as she gathered us around her.

'Daddy isn't coming home any more,' she simply said. But she added, between sobs, 'Mr Maguire knows more about this than meets the eye.' Words that stuck in my mind until nine years later when I sought the truth.

That day is forever imprinted on my brain and was to change the whole course of my life, my hopes, dreams and aspirations forever.

What was equally difficult for my mother was the fact that her father, my grandfather, had taken his own life the previous year. Apparently, he had been ill but had believed himself to be far worse than he was. I think this was a dreadful ending of life for a man who had survived the battle of The Somme. To spare my grandmother, he had taken an overdose. I firmly believe that my mother blamed my grandmother for this and later in life, I was quite saddened, and on occasions disgusted, by how she spoke to and behaved towards my grandmother.

Life from that day wasn't easy. My father's name was never mentioned by my mother for seven years—until I was 15 years old, and the full story of my father's death was never known to me until 40 years later, although when I was 17, I was regaled with snippets from both my grandmothers. Most of which were far from the truth.

My primary school teacher, Mrs Boston, was extremely compassionate and even had me to stay with her and her husband on one occasion. Unfortunately, she moved away from the area shortly afterwards although we did keep in touch by letter for a short while.

However, some children on the estate were far less compassionate and on several occasions, began taunting me with cries of "your mother's a widow". A word I had to ask my mother the definition of before I realised how cruel children can be to each other!

After a short while, even adults seemed cruel to me. One of our dinner ladies told me to stop crying as it was now more than two years since my father had died. But for me, even now, nothing can erase the grief and heartache I felt then and continued to feel for more than 40 years.

The financial blow was tremendous as although my father had taken out life insurance in 1957, in it, it stated that a suicide would not be paid out unless the policy had run for two years. Unfortunately, there were two more months to go! I also learned much later in life that until the early sixties, anyone who survived a suicide attempt was automatically hospitalised for several weeks. Later that year, on Christmas eve in fact, a school friend's father was killed while riding his motorbike leaving his mother with four boys. How life imitates itself.

My mother and the four of us then had to survive on a widow's pension as she was too proud, for whatever reason, to accept much help from either of my grandmothers. We did, of course, qualify for free school meals and the Local Authority gave us vouchers twice a year for a pair of shoes and a school coat.

Nanna (my father's mother) was an avid and competent knitter and we received some beautiful woollies to add to our sparse wardrobe and cast offs which somehow my grandma (my mother's mother) was able to acquire.

But the one redeeming feature about my mother, possibly, was that she kept us immaculately clean and the house was always spotless.

As always, after a bereavement, the "church", in some form or other, becomes visible—and so it was in our family's case. We received a visit from the vicar of St Johns and forthwith, we were enrolled in the Sunday school. I have to admit that it was in no way a chore as I relished collecting the beautifully coloured biblical stamps every week for attendance and it also meant that I was able to join the Brownies. I thoroughly enjoyed my time in the Brownies and obtained many achievement badges apart from also becoming a "sixer" before I finally left at the ripe old age of 11. The only bugbear about Brownies was that the uniform dictated that we wear black or brown shoes and at one point, I only possessed one pair of shoes which were red and, therefore, was frequently told I must speak to my mother about it which obviously under the circumstances was to no avail. Apart from the morning Sunday school, and I suppose to give my mother some more peace and quiet in the afternoon, we were sent to the Elim Church Sunday School. This was totally different to the rather staid and sombre morning service at St Johns and I enjoyed it immensely. There was a lot of singing, some of the songs I can still remember today and have in fact sung to my granddaughter. We actually learnt a great deal about the Bible and many wonderful stories of Jesus and his followers. There were exams which we could take depending on our age group and being as competitive as I was even at that tender age, I sat and passed very well indeed. There was a prize-giving after the examination results were made public and I still possess one or two of the books I was awarded as prizes.

The next three years of my life were fairly routine. I had to grow up very quickly. I learnt to iron and do some household chores and became a regular child minder, at eight years old, to my three younger sisters. Unfortunately, on one occasion, I let my youngest sister roll down a small hill as the brake on the buggy wasn't properly secured. She went smack into a wooden fence at the bottom and had the most almighty bruise which nothing could have hidden. Upon my return home, it was my grandma who had to rescue me from what would certainly have been a good hiding. My mother's outbursts of temper increased during these years and she let it out mostly on me, with whatever came to hand—a hairbrush, a hearth brush, even a cucumber! Nothing was sacred. There was also the terrifying threat of being taken into care if we didn't behave which she used as a verbal but nevertheless a fighting means of control. This was frequently used during those years.

During that time, an old friend, Tom, came to stay for a weekend. He was my mother's age and very handsome and personable. Years later, I asked her why she didn't marry him. She replied that she didn't feel he could have taken on 4 small children.

My mother had a very good friend in one of our neighbours and sometimes would accompany her to a local tombola session. We, however, were left in the house alone which nowadays would certainly have Social Services around investigating.

A great source of relief and release was to stay at either of my grandmother's for the weekend. Both having different but equally lovable attributes and both living alone. My mother's mother lived in a street, parallel to our old home, in an end terrace. However, her house possessed a bathroom and a very large garden of which she was immensely proud—but the toilet was still outside. Visiting her was always a pleasure. There was always something to help with in the garden and a swing on which I would soar high singing to myself. Bygone melodies such as *Around the World* and *Catch a Falling Star* and *Tulips from Amsterdam*, tunes I know are long since forgotten. She also had a piano in the front room which I was keen to play as by now, we no longer possessed a piano or indeed the finances for lessons.

On Saturday morning, we would go to the market but this often proved embarrassing as I was a shy, nervous child. My grandmother would look under every stall we passed and spy fallen treasures. An apple, orange, potato, carrot, banana, tomato or some other edible gem. Whilst she shielded me, I was to collect the said item and slip it into her shopping bag. She was absolutely delighted if we managed to collect half a bag full of bounty. I suppose times were hard then and she didn't really consider it stealing but my throat was dry and I visibly shook when capturing our prey. Another source of "income" was to send me round the streets with either bundles of sticks or rhubarb to sell to the neighbours.

In the evenings, we played cards or bagatelle and I was allowed to watch TV (black and white of course) and stay up much later than I would have been able to at home. I loved my grandmother dearly and always admired her courage and resilience and marvelled at the stories she had to tell. She had survived several monarchs, the Suffragette Movement, two World Wars and so many other fascinating things that were so interesting to listen to her talk about. She was incredibly active and was secretary of various OAP organisations until the age of 81 when she fell on coming home from one of her meetings and broke her hip. Unfortunately, she was never the same again and thereafter, it was a downward spiral physically. When she died at the age of 100, I felt that I had lost my last connection to the past and mysteries that would never be revealed to me.

My father's mother, called Nanna, to differentiate between the two, was the proud owner of a shop, which was originally the "front room". It was formerly a "pie and pea" shop when my father was young. Nanna opened the shop in order to single-handedly support her three children after her husband died at the young age of 32. By the time I was born, she had turned it into a corner shop, selling everything from food, drinks, tinned goods, cigarettes and small items of stationery and haberdashery. She opened six days a week and even when she was officially closed, neighbours would knock at the back door to be sold something in an "emergency".

If I was lucky enough to be there in the school holidays when the bread delivery van called, I would be allowed to travel to one or two other local shops in the cab which I found terribly exciting and for some reason, made me feel immensely grown up.

I loved being with Nanna too. Although she didn't have much of a garden, she too had a swing. But best of all was being able to have anything from the shop that I wanted. Sweets, ice cream, boiled ham for sandwiches, tins of Heinz soups and cherries. However, one day I over-indulged so much that I was violently sick and it was another 20 odd years before I could face vegetable soup again! Sunday evenings were lovely too. Nanna had two friends who lived a few doors away and they would come round to play cards for money. Only a few coppers (pennies) of course but it seemed a lot to me in those days. And a very special treat was the Odeon Cinema as Nanna received weekly free tickets for advertising on the shop's wall.

She always commemorated my father's birthday on the 30th December by having a New Year Eve's party for the family.

In the summer of 1960, my mother left my youngest sister with my grandma and took the remaining three of us on holiday to Ramsey on the Isle of Man. I don't remember too much about the trip except that in a playground, I decided to experience the highest slide I had ever seen but unfortunately I fell from the top causing such a horrendous nose bleed and shock that it really frightened my mother. She hailed a passing car who took us to the local hospital where I was kept overnight!

The following years, the holidays for two of my sisters and I were a fortnight at Filey Home in Primrose Valley, Filey, courtesy of the local council. The first time there were tearful farewells. It was a very scary time for us even though the three of us were together. We were accommodated in large dormitories, with one bathroom for girls and one for boys. Bath time was four in a bath at a time, something I never got used too. However, the food was plentiful if not wonderful and there was a tuck shop everyday if you had any money. Most days were spent on the beach or the cliff tops. We collected shells and bathed; I couldn't swim then, played group games, and in fact did have some good fun. If the weather was bad, there were board games to play or books to read. I don't know if the "Home" still exists perhaps not after all this time but at least it did provide a holiday for children whose parents couldn't afford one apart from the fact that it gave single parents respite from their children for two weeks.

During this period, my mother became acquainted with Mr Chatters. He was a good friend of my uncle and had lost his wife leaving him with two sons, both older than me. My uncle had introduced them at the works annual Christmas party to which we were all invited as my uncle paid for us since my father had died. At first, the relationship meant that we received spending money and treats. But children are instinctive and I had a bad feeling about the future. Also like most children would, I couldn't help comparing Mr C to my father and he always came up wanting in my eyes. Another "fly in the ointment" was his two sons. The eldest was uncouth, uneducated and downright obnoxious to my mother and things were to get worse.

However, in March 1962, my mother and Mr Chatters married and my life was thrown into turmoil again!

Chapter 2
A New Father and a
Sexual Assault

If things had been just about bearable before this date, they certainly took a dramatic change for the worse thereafter for some years to come. Upon returning home from school, one day we were suddenly to call Mr Chatters "Dad". The gross insensitivity of it! It pierced my heart as if someone had told me all over again that my father had died and I would no longer see him. I harboured dreams and fantasies that he had had to go away on some secret mission and he would return to claim me as his own beloved daughter and regale me with all his adventures and exploits of far-off lands.

The first change was that both families were to move in together in a large house which would accommodate all of us—two adults, two teenage boys and four girls between the ages of 4 and 11.

The property was a large stone-built house on the outskirts of the town several miles from where I currently lived and went to school. My new home seemed enormous—kitchen, dining room, living room, sitting room, five bedrooms, bathroom and three basement cellars. There was a small backyard but very little garden, as it was situated on a corner of two quite major roads. Sounds like a palace—but it was not. It was freezing cold as the ceilings were so high with no heating except a coal fire in the sitting room. It was draughty and it was very much in need of renovation. We were certainly cosy at night sleeping three or four in a bed! It was getting out in the mornings that was the problem! You could actually see your breath in front of you!

When we had moved into the house, it still needed a lot of work doing to it. In what was the old dining room was a dumbwaiter in one corner of the room. My sisters and I would often send our new baby sister visits down to the cellar and up again; fortunately, it doesn't appear to have traumatised her in any way.

Unfortunately, it was several miles from where I currently went to school. However, it was decided that with one term left, I would travel on two buses and walk until the end of the school year. My sisters transferred to the local primary school immediately.

That term was my first foray into the world of literature. There had been a poetry competition on the radio and our then teacher, Miss Richards, had submitted a selection of poems from our year. Imagine my surprise, as well as everyone else's, when mine was chosen to be read out on the radio. The classroom was hushed as a gentleman read out my entry. It was entitled "One-eyed Bill" and was a ghost story!

It was also during my last year at that primary school that I was fortunate enough to be allowed to go on a trip to London which was absolutely wonderful and very informative. Upon our return, we had to make a project folder and there was also a quiz in which I was in the winning team. I still have the project some 40 years later!

It was shortly after moving that we found the nearby park which was to become a favourite haunt of ours. It had a "castle" which had a small shop selling sweets and ice cream. In spring, the lightly wooded area and the hillsides were covered in bluebells. There was a bowling green, a football pitch and some well-cared-for gardens. It was on one of our excursions to collect wild flowers and bluebell bulbs for our little patch of garden that the incident occurred which I believe may have been the beginning of my future phobias.

My stepbrother, two younger sisters and I had just collected some flowers and I noticed a youth/man some distance away staring at us; I told my stepbrother that I was nervous, frightened even, but he said it wasn't a problem. I wanted to go home but he insisted that we carry on. However, after more persuasion, he agreed and we started to make our way back towards the park entrance across the flat grassy area above the bowling green.

Suddenly, a hand was thrust between my legs and an adult voice said, 'Nice cock you've got.' (He was obviously not too familiar with the female anatomy) I turned, I think we all did. I was staring into a face, which I will never forget even after 50 years. Slicked-back black hair and either frothing at the mouth or expunging so much saliva, black leather jacket and ice-blue jeans are all that I remember. I screamed and screamed and we all began to run towards the entrance. My sisters screamed but not my stepbrother. When we had reached the gates and safety, I looked back but there was no sign of him. We went home and never told a soul what had happened nor spoke of it again ourselves. How did you tell parents and adults in those days?

After that episode our "playground" was the playground and playing fields at Herringthorpe. It was where I had my first kiss at the age of 12 from a handsome boy called Chris. The first of many to be labelled with disapproval by my mother as "not suitable".

Back in the 60s, the 11+ examination still existed and passing it was a passport to a better education (as most people thought) for a pupil such as me coming from a somewhat financially limited background. Achieving academia on merit rather than by means of wealth, family name or connections has always seemed to me the best and indeed only way of being proud of the achievement.

And so it was that shortly after Easter I was informed (or rather my mother was) that I had passed the exam and would be beginning the September term at the Rotherham High School for Girls.

My nanna (my father's mother) and my auntie Dorothy (my father's sister) were thrilled for me and said that my father would have been extremely proud of me. Nanna had always said that for the first one of her grandchildren to pass the exam, she would buy them a new bicycle as a reward. Two days later nanna took me to the cycle shop where I chose a red and silver Raleigh bicycle. I was pleased as punch! My grandma (Mother's mom) bought me a real leather satchel which endured the whole time of my school days and my parents brought me a "Timex" watch. As always even the smallest happiness had to be marred. There was then the problem of finding money for a complete school uniform. However, that September, I duly arrived at the gates glad in a brand new school uniform. One of the advantages of the new house was that our neighbours had a daughter who was my age and she too passed the 11+ examination. We became friends and spent quite a lot of free time together in between all the teenage squabbles and fall-outs. We would play tennis in Clifton Park and pretend that we were Christine Trueman and Angela Mortimer but we spent most of the time picking up the balls and I'm not sure if we ever completed a game let alone a set! She also had a small pony which I was eventually persuaded to ride not wanting to be a sissy but I was petrified every time I was in the saddle.

Her mother, who became my new sister's godmother, was a member of a concert party and as Alison had several wonderful puppets, we were drafted in to produce a puppet show for the audience who loved it, but it was a most nerve-wracking experience for me. Her father had a very posh car, although I don't recall what make it was, and if I was lucky enough, I would sometimes have a lift to or from school.

I loved school and made several new friends but compared with the "crème de la crème" of Rotherham, I was only average but still enjoyed my time there. Home life I didn't enjoy much!

My stepbrothers had been spoiled since their mother died and had been indulged financially.

We were all given pocket money and my sisters and I used it to buy sweets. We never stole from home or shoplifted like some other children we knew. However, one night when we were all sleeping, my stepfather burst into the bedroom turning on the light. We all sat up in bed and watched in amazement as he proceeded to search all the drawers and wardrobes. Finding nothing, he left banging the door behind him.

In the fullness of time, it transpired that my youngest step brother had been stealing from home as well as school. As I have grown older, I have come to realise it was possibly to attract the attention he lacked after his mother died and his father remarried. Nevertheless, children can be very spiteful and my younger sisters and I revelled in playing tricks on him. These ranged from "apple pie" beds to hiding his belongings and later on to having various things posted to the house in his name. Shortly after this my eldest stepbrother married and myself and his fiancee's 'sister were bridesmaids. We wore cherry red velvet dresses trimmed with white fur as it was a December wedding.

About 18 months after her wedding, my mother became pregnant. My eldest stepbrother was disgusted for some reason, perhaps the thought of his father having had sex. We were told that the new baby would be adopted as we were already a "full-house" and couldn't afford another mouth to feed. My mother told me much later that she had done everything she could to "get rid of it". My sister was duly born and started her life in a makeshift cot. It was the drawer of a wardrobe resting on two chairs, borrowed from our next-door neighbours. We were all summoned that morning before school to welcome the new arrival. Days later, a lady arrived at our front door, obviously someone who didn't know us or an official, as it was never used. Apparently, she was calling about my sister. However, my stepfather sent her packing. We were all summoned again shortly afterwards and told that our new sister would be staying and we would all have to make sacrifices as there was another person to take care of. When you think things are bad and can't get any worse, in my experience, they always do!

Circumstances, therefore, dictated that from the early age of 12, I had to find ways of funding almost everything I needed or wanted. We did, however, receive weekly pocket money depending on age and we had an annual increase on our birthdays. A lot of it was saved with which to buy birthday, Easter and Christmas presents, as a family we always remembered and celebrated these events religiously. The rest was used to buy sweets at the local shop after Sunday school and eat them while watching the afternoon film.

My first job was a paper round; there was no minimum age until recently. It was difficult sometimes, particularly in the winter. It was dark and freezing cold so early in the morning and I had to be back in time to get ready for school. Often in the holidays, other children would not turn up and I ended up doing sometimes three rounds. All that kept me going, when I felt utterly desperate, was the money at the end of the week. I was very good at needlework and made clothes for myself and my young sisters. Another entrepreneurial idea came from my grandmother. Nylon-knitted coat hanger covers were very popular, non-slip and I could literally churn out at least six a week.

Seasonal money-spinners were carol singing and going door-to-door with holly which I edged with silver or gold paint. Not too much outlay there as the holly came from the local hedgerows, well a doctor's garden and of course "penny for the guy" and "trick or treat".

I was also a Saturday girl in a local hairdresser and eventually graduated to working in Woolworths on the broken biscuit counter. That was when you really had to be good at mental arithmetic, no computerised tills then. By this time, I was totally self-sufficient and I believe the only thing my parents bought me from the age of 14 was a coat which I detested immensely and felt embarrassed to wear.

It was about that time that I acquired a French penfriend. We exchanged letters for several months until the French teacher told me that she and her family would be coming to England for a holiday and would like Marie Claire to stay with my family for a few days. I was delighted when my mother agreed to this. What was more surprising was that my mother bought various fruits and set them in full view on the coffee table in the sitting room. I think it was the first time my sisters and I had ever seen so much fruit except in magazines or the market!

It was during this time that Rotherham was still a thriving, albeit, small town. We had three cinemas, two department stores and a variety of "good" shops.

My friends used to meet on Saturday mornings for a coffee and to window shop but of course I was at home doing my chores. Real shopping was always done in Sheffield anyway, normally at C&A. Such a pity a lot of the shops suffered when MeadowHall opened its doors many years later.

There was not an awful lot to do but there was a Wimpey bar, no MacDonald's, KFC, Starbucks or the like. It was most certainly like the aftermath of the pit and steel closures portrayed in *The Full Monty*, a film which I must have watched at least 30 times!

Chapter 3
Teenage Years

My teenage years were very unlike those of most of my contemporaries. When friends were meeting on Saturday morning for coffee and shopping, I was at home doing housework. Even in the week, we all had to help out, washing-up, drying, peeling mountains of potatoes and ironing. We even had a rota!

School was my escape but that wasn't always true. I was chosen for one of the school hockey teams but after playing only a handful of matches, I had to decline as I was needed on Saturday mornings at home. Likewise, with the tennis team in the summer—I only played two matches. They too were on a Saturday morning.

Nevertheless, I found an outlet of release which originally began as somewhat of a chore.

When we moved to the area, we were all sent to the local Methodist chapel, morning and afternoon. The morning service had a short morning Sunday school during the adult service and again at 2:30, there was Sunday school. It was one way to get the children out of the house for most of the day. However, there were friends and companionship and I do remember those times with fondness.

In December 1964, I was chosen to be Mary in the nativity play and as my sister was almost five months old, we approached my mother with a view to using her as the baby Jesus. And she actually agreed. Imagine the audience's reaction when hearing my sister make baby noises and actually cry.

It was probably the best nativity play anyone had seen. If only for that reason. Mother's Day was a triumph for the family. Most families received one or, at most, two flowers, our mother received a whole bunch, all six of them! One great advantage of attending Sunday school regularly was the Friday night youth club. Several of my school friends came on Sundays just to be members of the youth club.

We played music, even danced sometimes. There was pop and crisps and, naturally, boys.

My first real boyfriend was a member but it didn't last long nor did many others after that. I wasn't very mature physically and I didn't want to be groped behind the church!

Sometimes we helped at events such as jumble sales. One particular one was a hoot. The doors were opened and the rush was incredible. This particular time one of the boys took off his jacket only to see, minutes later, an old man wearing it and asking the price. Needless to say, it took ages to persuade him that it wasn't for sale!

Running away at the age of 14 was one thing I regret and wish I could change. I had been chosen for a German exchange program but unfortunately in a fit of anger at the way I was treated compared to one of my younger sisters, I ran away from home (only for two nights) and stayed with a school friend and I don't think I was even missed! The trip was cancelled and I had the humiliation and embarrassment of telling the German teacher.

The Sunday school's one, and I believe only, claim to fame was one WhitsunTide (Now called Spring Bank/May Bank I believe). Decorated floats from all the different churches in the area gathered at the old fairground and then proceeded through the streets to Clifton Park where they were judged. We knew ours was good—so much thought and effort had gone into it. We even had one of the young men of the congregation playing the organ as our float made its triumphant progress towards Clifton Park. We won!!!—a triumph for the young of the church.

It was not long after this that I was asked to become a Sunday school teacher. It meant spending Tuesday evening, with another teacher in the primary department, at a senior teacher's home. This was to go through the lesson for the following Sundays and the order of service and hymns and stories and activities for the children. I found it reasonably easy to deal with my small group but when called upon to address the whole class, I was a bag of nerves even with several months of practice. This was partly due to the fact that the senior teacher was very strict and most of the children were a little afraid of her. However, after a short time of getting to know her better I began to like her very much and we became good friends.

When I married and moved away we corresponded regularly and she eventually married a colleague from work and was very happy.

We met again some years later when I was invited to open the church's annual fete.

The family was now, however, fortunate enough to have annual summer holidays. It was always "stock weeks". That was the last week in July and the first week in August when the steel works virtually closed down for two weeks. We would always rent a house on the coast somewhere fairly local. I do remember a holiday in Mablethorpe with fondness, if only because there was a funfair there and I became infatuated with the young man who worked on the Ferris wheel and paid to go on it so many times even though I was terrified of heights and hated every second that I was on it!

One year we actually ventured further afield to Ramsgate or Margate, I can't recall which but I do know it was full of French exchange schoolchildren, where we practiced our dreadful schoolgirl French.

Rolling Stones + Mick Jagger + Donovan

I think the highlight of my teenage years was seeing the Rolling Stones live at Sheffield City Hall third row seats. The late Brian Jones even picked up a gonk I had thrown on to the stage. However, I had a sore throat for three days after that from all the screaming! Imagine my delight when over 30 years later, I met Mick Jagger at a BAFTA awards ceremony and actually shook his hand and spoke to him. What a gentleman even though he must get sick of all the attention.

My other excursion to the City Hall in Sheffield was to see Donovan. I was much luckier on this occasion, or not, as I was able to mount the stage and touch my idol before being brutally thrown off by one of the "bouncers". It meant that I had my arm in a sling for a couple of weeks afterwards but it was worth it!

There weren't too many places for young people to go in Rotherham. Pubs were out of bounds and even though there were actually three cinemas at that time in the town, money was always an issue. However, on Saturday nights, there was a club in the basement of the Parish Church Hall which anyone who was anyone had to be seen in, or even the YMCA.

Unfortunately, due to the fact that I had to be home by 9:30, even at 15/16, by the time I had queued to get in, it was almost time for me to go home. This made me feel like a leper with almost all my friends.

Pete Stringfellow

It was when I was 16 that I first had occasion to meet the famous, or is it infamous, Pete Stringfellow. I had won a competition in the local newspaper to meet "The Move" and supposedly have dinner with them at the Brentwood Hotel. I was the outright winner and had been promised an evening with the group. Unfortunately, just 15 minutes before I was due to leave for the location, I was informed that they were unable to make it. The rendezvous was rescheduled for a Sunday afternoon at the "Mojo" Club in Sheffield but unhappily for me, several other fans were invited to massage the group's ego.

It is very strange to think that more than 30 years later, my son admired Pete so greatly, and still does, that he wanted to follow in his footsteps and has indeed followed his colourful career since his late teens. In fact, he has made a pretty good job of emulating him both in his business dealings, and much to my ex-husband's chagrin, in his personal life too! I didn't get much chance to chat given that at that time I was quite a timid teenager and the other invitees were all probably future models. However, I did manage to acquire a drumstick (not the chicken variety luckily) from Bev Bevan. I do believe there was a reporter from the newspaper but I don't recall any photographs being taken. Perhaps Pete has some!

I did have several boyfriends during my teenage years at home but they all wanted to have sex and I was more afraid of my mother than becoming pregnant. Her attitude always amazed me since I was born only six months after she married! The nearest I came to "going all the way" was with "Rex". He was a grammar school boy who so many girls literally drooled over. I went around with him for three months until one evening after a heavy petting session, I actually let him get into my pants but then I chickened out. The next day, he sent his best friend to tell me that we were finished as there were plenty of girls who would have sex with him. I'm sure there were but at the time I couldn't be one of them.

I had always wanted to be a teacher when I left school and I was to take 10 "O" levels in the summer of 1967. I still believe that these were a much harder exam to pass than the current GCSCs, having taken both.

My mother made an appointment to see my headmistress which was a first as she had never once been to any of my parent's evenings. I was later told that if I studied hard, I would be allowed to stay on to take "A" levels and there would be financial assistance.

But it was not to be. Shortly after, my mother told me that my stepfather would not let me continue my education and I would have to start work. Looking back with hindsight and more experience of her underhand nature, I believe it was she that decided and not him.

However, as it was I didn't pass all the 10 "O" levels, I became ill in the early spring of that year and actually started coughing blood. I didn't even smoke then. I was referred to a consultant and informed that I had a patch on my left lung, which would necessitate being admitted to the local sanatorium for at least a few weeks, I was devastated as we were due to go on holiday at that time and my two younger sisters and I had planned to see the Tremeloes in concert.

I was admitted to the sanatorium and the rest of the family went on holiday without me. I had visits from my nanna and various other relatives as well as Reverend Webster from the chapel. I was rooming with an African woman called Angelina who had tuberculosis and we struck up a friendship. She had six children and was looking for a nanny/mother's help when she would be eventually allowed home. I seriously considered the offer but of course my mother was against it, perhaps rightly on this occasion.

I, therefore, applied to numerous banks and after several interviews and exams was fortunate enough to secure a position with Williams and Deacons, no longer in existence, in the town centre.

As a junior, my most important tasks were making the morning coffee and the afternoon teas. There was some respite, however, in the form of hand delivering the local mail and doing shopping for the senior staff. It was from one of the older women at work that I thought I had learnt about childbirth. During a discussion, one of them was heard to say, 'I wouldn't want any man to see me have my bowels opened.' I was then under the firm impression that babies were delivered via one's anus!

It was at the bank that I met my next semi-serious boyfriend, Martin, but after a few months, that ended too because of my failure to have sex with him. It was the age of Flower Power and Free Love but nothing in this world is free, there is always a price to pay in some way or another. So Free Love passed me by as did the CND as my parents were very much against the movement for some reason although one of my friend's brothers was heavily involved. It wasn't until much later in life that I actually knew what they stood for, if I had known, I would have been right along with them.

My next semi-serious boyfriend was an equal disaster but for a very different reason. He was several years older than me and had been going around with one of my younger sister's teachers. The moment she heard of our association, she began bullying and picking on my sister. Although this was normally my mother's job, she did not want anyone else to do the same to any member of her brood. She was up at the school like a shot and although none of us can be completely certain what went on between them, my sister was from that moment treated with great respect and I lost a boyfriend!

Although, I enjoyed having a monthly salary and being able to keep up with the latest fashions and music. I was still very unhappy at my lack of freedom and my mother's constant mood changes although it had been a few years since I had experienced her physical outbursts. The last time it was because I went to the shops with a friend without telling her.

When I arrived home, she proceeded to beat me about the head and face, all the time I was trying to get up the stairs.

My nose was bleeding and it was actually my stepfather who halted the proceedings.

Since beginning work at the bank, all I could think about was leaving home by any means possible. I researched all branches of H.M.F. The RAF was discounted as I had never flown and flying did not appeal, seeming unnatural. How could such a large metal contraption full of people even take off the ground. Little did I know then how flying would become one of my greatest phobias. The navy was discounted as previously mentioned I had only obtained three GCSEs.

The army was the most sensible and viable option. To this end, I duly attended interviews, selection testing and medicals in Sheffield. Strange as it may seem, now at the medical, I was advised to put on a little weight as I was below eight stone! (And was until the age of 34 when I was pregnant with my second child).

During the course of the form filling, I had to state that my father was deceased. This brought back memories and opened up old wounds and mysteries. I decided to go along to the local library and managed to view old newspapers from July 1959, one was entitled "Mystery Death of Star Cricketer".

I decided to try to obtain a copy of my father's death certificate but for whatever reason in those days, a policeman was on duty at the registry office and after explaining what I was there for, he promptly sent me home to "talk to my family". I found the nearest phone box and looked up the number for Arthur Lee and Son. Having been answered by a female I asked to speak to Mr Maguire. 'Putting you through,' the voice said. At which I hastily slammed down the receiver, still shaking, my head pounding. So HE still worked there after nine years but my father was dead! I decided to call on my paternal grandmother, Nanna. My aunt, my father's sister, and my cousin were there too. I said I wanted to know what really happened to my father. My grandmother and aunt said it had been a terrible accident and that he had, whilst in the laboratory, drunk potassium cyanide instead of his tea. I must always believe it was an accident they said. What else would they say?

My next visit was to my maternal grandmother, Grandma. She was more forthcoming and as it turned out more honest. She said it wasn't an accident but that he had been very troubled. My parent's marriage was not ideal, my mother was always nagging him, he had disliked work more and more and it was a spur of the moment thing. Although I was later to find out more than 40 years later that even this wasn't the whole truth!

Due to the absence of my father, my stepfather's signature was necessary, as I was still only 17, to enable me to finally enlist. My mother said she had to persuade him but I'm sure he was glad to "see the back of me". A thorn in his side. I remember saying goodbye to family and friends and promising to write. My class at Sunday school, where I was a primary teacher, said goodbye too. That was sad. I have always, and still do, love children. It was many years later that I returned to that church in order to open their annual fete.

Chapter 4
Leaving Home and Germany

I set off to the station early one morning in April, my destination being Guildford. No one had come to see me off but what had I expected—a tearful farewell perhaps? My heart was pounding as I boarded the train. My head was a mélange of feelings: excitement, fear, loneliness and sadness. But how could my future be anymore lonely or sad than the past I had left behind that morning.

There are certain things I can remember quite vividly but that journey and the following hours before arriving in Guildford are quite hazy, perhaps I slept for most of the journey. Upon arrival, I was shown my room (billet) which I was to share with three other recruits. At least I didn't have to share a bed! I was also overjoyed at the sight of the ablutions which meant that I could take a shower or have a bath at any time or day I wanted to without having to have a special day of the week or queue for the toilet! I had decided, when asked, to use my second Christian name (give name—now to be politically correct) Leaving behind the past and hopefully its miseries.

A new name—a new life. I couldn't have been happier. I loved the camaraderie, even enjoyed the discipline, but most of all, the freedom when off duty.

Saturday night was "the" night. A night at the Naafi in Aldershot—a train ride away, but a journey to another world. Drinking, dancing and an abundance of men! In those days, I was slim, attractive and up to the date. Fashion-wise, I could have my pick of anyone there. I was spotted by a blond-haired Adonis, belonging to the parachute regiment but he was obviously older than me and I declined his advances. At the end of the evening, exhausted from dancing but very happy, I caught the train back to camp. I was alone as friends had teamed up for the evening but I was still shy and wary of this new free environment. Just as the train was about to pull away from the station, the fair-haired Adonis jumped into the carriage beside me.

I hadn't had any alcohol but I could tell that he had been drinking, not too much though. The journey passed quickly as we exchanged idle banter and witticisms and at the end, I found myself agreeing to meet him again. Instead of the crowded Naafi, he took me to a quiet pub where we chatted easily and I realised I was won over by his charm and with, not to mention, his incredible good looks. He walked me back to the station and having found a secluded spot out of the glare of the platform lights he began to kiss me. At first, he was gentle and loving but he soon became more passionate and his hands tried to find my breasts and the inside of my thighs. I froze. Telling him 'NO' didn't help. He had wrongly assumed that I was easy. 'All the other WRACs are,' he almost shouted. In a few seconds, he had turned from being my handsome Adonis to a lecherous monster. I struggled free and straightened my clothing. Even explaining that I was a virgin didn't seem to cut any ice. He just didn't seem to believe me. He turned and walked slowly away and I was left to wait for my train alone. I was quite miserable on the way home and thought about him for the whole of the following week. When Saturday finally came, I was sure he would have changed this mind, but no. He was there drinking with friends and barely acknowledged me. With hindsight, I realise it was total infatuation with the person I thought he was. But I was determined to win him over. I wrote to him explaining how I felt and my reasons for refusing him that night but I later learnt from a friend of his that he had pinned my letter on the notice board for all to see. Thus, ending any further liaisons with anyone in Aldershot.

At this point, I began to feel very homesick and thought I had made a terrible mistake. But what was there to go back to? Although! The reason I left in the first place.

After my basic training, the kit cleaning and the parade drills it was time for my "Passing Out Parade". Needless to say, there was no one there from my family to watch that or my platoon winning the drill competition.

Shortly afterwards, I was posted to Catterick Camp and joined the R.S. Corps. The training was intense but enjoyable. The accommodation wasn't luxurious as Guilford but the camp was mixed! Training was exacting and there were numerous tests and exams to pass but it was extremely interesting and thoroughly worthwhile I even went on an outward-bound course to Lake Ullswater, where I actually managed abseiling, shooting and being tipped out of a canoe in the middle of the lake to swim to shore! Oh to be young again!

Nightlife once again revolved around the Naafi and there was a glut of men to choose from as there were not only the ones stationed there but the ones on camp for upgraded training from all parts of the globe.

It was there that I met Danny, extremely tall, fit and handsome and so many other girls fancied him. He was fashionable, when in civvies, smart in uniform, witty and up-to-date with all the latest music which I was in 1968! After a few weeks together, we arrange a weekend away at the coast with several friends.

It was under canvas on a cliff top in Scarborough that I lost my virginity to Danny. I can honestly say it was the most painful experience of my life up to that point—and so much blood. It was more painful than childbirth. At least after that I had something to love and cherish. The experience left me disillusioned and wondering for years why sex was such a big issue in a relationship. Perhaps if he hadn't been a virgin too, things might have been different. Nevertheless, our relationship continued until he returned to Germany. I even travelled to Enfield to meet his family and there was talk of marriage. When Danny returned to Germany after his course had finished, I used to stay in bed in the evenings and at weekends remaining totally faithful. Little did I know that he wasn't! The only events I can recall during this time were being pursued during the day, perhaps to ascertain whether I was the unfaithful type, and something I will never forget was when several of my roommates gave a girl a regimental bath.

At the end of my training, to my great delight, I received a posting to Germany. Beforehand, however, I was to be involved in a NATO exercise for 10 days. One or two of my course mates were going too. There was the excitement of my first passport, packing and speculating about what Germany would be like. My first trip out of Britain. We flew from Manchester Airport—Runways. It was certainly nothing like the enormous international airport it is now. I don't recall too much except the horrendous noise of the engines and being absolutely petrified!

We were met at Dusseldorf and driven to our quarters at Rheindahlen where everyone was amazingly friendly and we were given our first 24 hrs free. We were introduced on our first night to German nightlife which was quite unlike anything at a Naafi. We went to a real nightclub with brilliant music and lights and even more brilliant talent. We spotted two gorgeous German men who kept eyeing us up even though they were with two girls. Obviously we encouraged them. The next day, I was on a night shift and the following morning, totally exhausted, I slept from 8 am until 1 pm. When I woke, I was told that the two German guys from our first night were in the same club and one was looking for me. Bad luck for being tired—I never bumped into him again. A few days later in a different club, I met Ulli (Ullrich). He was a classic Arian German with a red sports car, quite a catch at my age.

He seemed quite smitten with me and even though our conversations were not too deep and meaningful (my 'O' level German wasn't great having failed but it was still better than his non-existent English!). I was invited for a meal to meet his parents. I managed to tell them my father worked in the steelworks. *Mein vater arbeitet im stahlwerks* (I think that's right!).

When I returned to England, I was sent on leave before returning to Germany to begin my posting. A day or so after I had been home, my mother summoned me into the "lounge". I couldn't immediately guess what she wanted to say but it all became clear when I saw an envelope in her hand. It was addressed to me of course—she had always been in the habit of opening our mail and/or even destroying it. It had been from Danny in Germany (I hadn't been unfaithful to him by the way.) In it, he referred to the fact of being a virgin. I had hung on to my virginity until having left home and then as now I always failed to understand her puritanical views when she herself had succumbed. She, as always played on the fact that upsetting her caused her health problems—she's still the creaking, moaning gate to this day. She wrote to my commanding officer and as the legal age of adulthood was 21 and her wishes for my "best interests" had to be considered and my posting to Germany was duly cancelled. I was held in Guildford until another posting could be found.

It wasn't any of the exotic places I had envisaged, it was Hounslow and I would be working in Whitehall. Nevertheless, I was determined to make the most of it. Yet again the accommodation was hardly even two-star but the friends I made there compensated for it and the work in the city was interesting and enjoyable and made more so by the people I worked with.

We had fun even when on duty—making prank calls while operating the switchboard, sneaking out of ground floor windows to collect takeaway food and generally having a good time.

There were no clubs or the kind of nightlife I had been used to but my next "companion" came in the shape of Colin who was a civilian decorator on camp. He had a scooter which again was an attraction. He lived fairly locally with his parents and was an only child.

I met his parents and used to visit frequently and it wasn't long before our relationship was sealed in his single bed.

I was due a visit to Yorkshire so I decided to take Colin with me. We travelled all the way from the south by scooter. Quite a hair raising, not to say, very long, journey. He stayed at my home but I duly dragged him round all the relatives. Due to the fact we could carry very little luggage, I washed our "smalls" and socks before we left. A big mistake! My mother decided that if you did that for a man, you were naturally intimate! After another lecture, we departed back to the south under a great black cloud—not just a rain cloud. Several weeks later, I was called into the CO's office to be told I had been posted to Singapore. My mother certainly put distance between me and another suitor this time. Part of me was sad but the bigger part of me was quite excited about travelling to the Far East. There were numerous vaccinations and yet more good-byes to family and friends.

This time I flew from Brize Norton. In those days, 1969, the journey was over 32 hours including stop-offs. By the time we arrived, I had almost, but not quite, become accustomed to flying.

Chapter 5
Far East Posting and Raped

Stepping out of the plane, I was hit by the sudden warmth and unfamiliar smells of an eastern country. It seemed, and was, thousands of miles from the dull, cold October England I had left behind 36 hours ago. I was met and escorted to a small army vehicle, I don't ever remember by whom now. The journey to the barracks was full of alien sights and sounds and smells and I felt a certain amount of trepidation. I shouldn't have worried since inside the barracks, surrounded by fellow squaddies, I felt completely at home. I found out shortly after my arrival that it had been the location for that excellent Film *The Virgin Soldiers*, although I certainly don't remember many virgins during my time there!

The accommodation wasn't quite what I was used to but it didn't matter. It was adequate and this was the beginning of a new chapter in my life. My fellow roommate, as there were two empty beds waiting to be filled, was four years my senior at 22 and from the first moment I met her, I was captivated by her self-assurance and worldly knowledge. She knew all the dodges and was more than willing to initiate me. She also knew how to take care of herself, and me at times. That first night lying in bed talking to Angela I raised my eyes to the ceiling, well rafters really as there was an 18" gap between the top of the walls and the roof. My heart missed a beat. There was a snake about 4ft long hanging over a beam, dangling either side. Catching my breath and remaining calm, well more or less I explained to Angela as best I could between gulps of breath. Quite calmly and matter-of-factly, she said, 'Pull the covers over your head and go to sleep. It will be gone in the morning.' I don't know how long it took me to get to sleep but sure enough, in the morning, it was gone. My second encounter with a snake was much scarier. With only a towel wrapped around me and wash-bag in hand, I proceeded to the communal bathrooms. As I stooped to put in the plug and turn on the taps, I came face to face with an extremely long, enormously fat snake. The likes of which I had never seen before. I even shudder at the thought of it now. Slowly stepping backwards, I reached the door and ran screaming for help. Help was indeed at hand in the form of our regimental sergeant major, who, broom handle in hand, proceeded to beat the offending reptile into another world.

I really loved my time in Singapore, the weather was great and it was a different world. The melting pot of cultures, the nightlife and the men, of all different nationalities all of whom seemed well off compared to a humble squaddie. The down side was that Levi's jeans and Ben Sherman shirts with red braces were no longer acceptable as part of my wardrobe. Trousers were a no at any time on base as it gave the wrong impression but we had local dressmakers who called every week and could make anything from a picture or a drawing at very reasonable prices.

The nightlife was amazing compared to what I had left behind in "Blighty". There were bars, restaurants, clubs, discos and always the spectacle of the street markets. Dozen s of stalls with a whole manner of foods being cooked in metal pots in the open air. There were other stalls too which sold various trinkets at ridiculous prices, everything seemed so cheap and affordable after England.

After a couple of weeks there, I decided that it was time that I did something positive about birth control. That was my first mistake. I made an appointment with the MO who was a woman. However, upon telling her that I had come to ask to be put on the pill, she gave me a lecture about sex before marriage and promptly sent me packing.

But as usual, Angela came to the rescue. She was on the pill and used to buy it from a small Chinese chemist downtown. She took me the following day and that was me sorted. Let the fun begin!

My first liaison was with a very dishy corporal. He was intelligent, funny and good fun to be with. We were invited to a party given by one of his senior NCOs and, of course, it meant that I needed an SOP (sleeping out pass). These weren't too difficult to obtain. Usually one of the married soldiers on one's shift would write a letter saying that you were babysitting and staying overnight. Occasionally however, they had to be forged! It was at this particular party that disaster struck. Everyone had had a lot to drink, including me. I somehow lost contact with Scott and feeling extremely sick and dizzy decided to head for the bathroom which was upstairs. Having been to the loo and washed my face, trying to sober up, I crashed out in one of the bedrooms. I can't remember how much later it was that I was awakened by a body on top of me kissing me feverishly. I was so far gone that I didn't have the strength to do anything. The next minute I was having sex although I prefer to describe it as being raped while in a drunken stupor. As soon as he had finished, he left and I struggled to pull myself together. When I got downstairs, I found Scott who asked me where I had been, so I know it wasn't him!

After that, our relationship lasted only a couple of weeks as I couldn't cope with the shame or embarrassment of him inadvertently finding out even though I was the victim.

My next beau was an equally dishy American on R and R from Vietnam (there were many of them at that time). My friends were quite jealous as they said he looked like Warren Beatty. We never had sex; he just wanted to rest and relax before returning to Vietnam.

Sometimes, Angela and I would head to the bar in the Cathy Hotel. It was a hangout for the well-off American workers and obviously guests of the hotel. One of Angela's stunts was to order drinks and put the bill on to any room number she could think of. Funnily enough, we were never questioned, so it was a cheap night out! Angela and I used to frequent a club on Orchard Road that had great music and on this particular occasion, two "gorgeous guys" were there together. The case was usually that one was OK and the other crap! After dancing for a while but keeping a close eye on our "prey", we went to the bar to order drinks. Obviously, we decided to stand right next to them, knowing full well that they had been eyeing us up, they asked us what we wanted to drink and we spent the evening with them. Luckily, Angela and I had picked the same ones who had-picked us. I ended up with Mike, a tall blond American who was a diver for a locally based outfit. Dave, slightly shorter and dark-haired, was also an American diver with the same company. As he was saying goodbye to Angela, he said, 'I would like to have an affair with you.' Nothing like coming straight to the point! We both made dates for later on in the week and went back to barracks very pleased with ourselves. And so my relationship with Mike began.

He worked on a rig somewhere off Jakarta and was often away but when he was in town, I would spend time at his flat which was just a few hundred yards from the beach. I loved having somewhere to cook and a private bathroom apart from all the attention he gave me and the occasional present. However, on our first night in bed together, he must have assumed I was a virgin as he said, 'Don't be frightened, I won't hurt you.' Little did he know, but he soon found out.

We would swim in the sea most times that I visited and once he even taught me to scuba dive. It was somewhat scary at first but being able to see all the brightly coloured fish and the incredible sea-life compensated for the initial fear. It was the first time that I experienced sex in the sea. Luckily we were far enough away from the beach for only the fish to see!

Shortly after that, we went on a trip over the Causeway into Malaysia with friends on a water-skiing trip. Unfortunately, I didn't fare so well at that.

As it happened, his family were in Singapore as his father was an overseas journalist and I was invited to celebrate Thanksgiving with them at their home. It was a lovely evening and his younger sister and I arranged to meet up later for a shopping trip.

Although I was pretty keen on Mike, I couldn't turn into a nun when he was away so there were others, normally just dates for a meal or a night out. One evening, I met a rather gorgeous Italian airline pilot who was staying at the famous Raffles Hotel. After a wonderful meal in the restaurant, we retired to his room. But after being forced, for the first time, into anal sex, it was the first and last time we ever met!

However, on one of our visits to the Cathay Hotel, I met Harry. Another American diver who worked for a different company to Mike. He was much older than me at 33 and had been married. He was a lot more experienced than me and was always giving me advice in bed which I found rather humiliating and made me feel incredibly naive. Nevertheless, he was a kind and generous escort when Mike was on the rig. Unfortunately, matters came to a head when all three of us were invited to the same party! The upshot was that Mike left with his friend and didn't call for two days. But professing his love for me, he forgave me and that was the end of Harry and anyone else, I became a one-man woman for the rest of my time in Singapore.

It was Mike that introduced me to "pot". The first time it made me feel incredibly giddy and light-headed and eventually sick but the more times I tried it, the better it seemed to get, although that wasn't too often.

Singapore was also my first brush royalty. The duchess of Kent was on the island and was visiting various locations on her tour. I was one of the ones chosen to be presented to her. We had a couple of rehearsals and we were told what to say when we were introduced. However, nerves got the better of me and I forgot the correct procedure and just shook hands and mumbled, 'Pleased to meet you.' Needless to say, she didn't remain to carry on a conversation with me!

It was impossible to spend the entire night out as bed-check was at midnight and strictly enforced; however, Angela being Angela, found a way round everything. Ten minutes or so after we thought the coast was clear, we would put a chair against the fence and throw the small carpet over the barbed wire. One of us would then give the other a leg-up and then over and drop down to the other side. This meant a walk along a long lane in the pitch dark until the main road was reached but it was worth it. Getting back in the morning was just a matter of going into breakfast and then back to one's room. I did this many times to spend the night with Mike. Many others did this and no one ever seemed to get caught. Perhaps it wasn't really a secret after all.

One evening, I fell asleep and was late back to sign in and had to pay the penalty. Several nights on duty in the guardroom.

Angela was always game for anything and one night we sneaked into the open-air swimming pool to skinny dip. We were caught by the duty staff sergeant major of our shift. Fortunately, he had a huge crush on Angela even though he was a married man with children. Needless to say, we got away with the escapade but not before he had an eyeful of me getting out of the water!

I used to write home to family and did receive some letters although they seemed to take ages. I would tell my younger sisters all my news but I have a feeling that my mother used to read them too. It was a big mistake to have told them about Mike as I later came to regret it. He had asked me to marry him before I would have to return to England but as the age of consent was still 21, I needed parents' permission. Mike contacted the American embassy but that was a blow too.

He had been unable to be called up for Vietnam as it was believed that he had some sort of a blood disorder, but unfortunately there had been a mistake and the embassy was apparently trying to trace him to sort things out.

In the meantime, my mother had written to yet another commanding officer, stating that she was unhappy with my current relationship and I had lecture about "parents only wanting the best" etc. particularly my mother. I don't think so! Mike was on the rig at that time so I decide that the only thing to do was to go AWOL, but that too was a big mistake. I was hiding out at his flat when two military police came looking for me. There was no point trying to hide or make a fuss so I just collected a few of my things and left a note for Mike.

When I was returned to the barracks, I was put under open arrest which meant that I couldn't leave my accommodation except for work.

The following day, I was told that I was being sent back to Guildford, England, to a holding company. I had to pack my belongings in haste and leave behind the things that were at Mike's flat.

Angela and I said a tearful goodbye and I was escorted to Changi Military Base where I was put on to, well actually, into an RAF Hercules plane, that being the earliest transport available. It was like being part of the cargo with wooden seats and mesh netting. Obviously, we couldn't reach the UK without stopping to refuel and we landed for several hours in Bahrain. I believe I had formulated my plan during the journey and when we landed in Bahrain, I feigned illness as I was just recovering from a kidney infection (no, on this occasion it isn't too much sex!). The plane took off without me whilst the resident MO (medical officer) said I needed fluids and rest. How wonderful! I stayed in really good accommodation with great food and spent the week sunbathing in the daytime and drinking in the bar at night with fellow residents. But as all good things must come to an end, I was booked on a passenger flight leaving after six days. I felt sure that there would be the military police waiting to meet me in the UK. What could I do?

But fate lent a hand again. One of the stewards on the flight was travelling up to Lincoln when he finished his shift. After de-planning, I hid in the ladies toilet until the coast was clear and then off up the motorway to Lincoln with my "white knight". He kindly dropped me at the station where I caught a train to Rotherham. I didn't go home. I went straight to Nanna's of course.

I stayed with her for a few days until she politically suggested that I should go to see my mother. As soon I arrived home, my mother said that police had been to the house in search of me and I was to give myself up voluntarily which I did two days later. When I reported to the guardroom, I was in civvies. After refusing to put on a uniform as everything was in transit, I was locked up in a cell for the night. Three nights went on like this as I kept insisting I wanted to purchase my discharge. However, it was a stalemate and I reluctantly donned my uniform and settled into H&D Company. Not without punishment of course. Days and days of "jankers". Mostly in the kitchens cleaning or in the bathrooms.

Chapter 6
Two Lesbian Affairs

I had decided that life in the forces in England would be decidedly unexciting and with this in mind, I determined to purchase my discharge. I was to remain in a holding company until my future was decided. After having spent nine months in the Far East I was tanned, lithe lonely, impressionable and easy prey to the many gay soldiers on camp. At first, I resisted all advances clinging to the hope that I would return to Singapore and the waiting Mike as we had spoken on the telephone and he had sent me the money for the airfare back to Singapore. But the weeks dragged on and the loneliness wore me down. I was only able to speak to Mike on a couple of occasions due to the fact that he was either on the rig or a connection couldn't be made. It was after all 1970 and the technology was nothing like it is today. Nights in the Naafi were my only entertainment and after the bar closed, the lights were turned down and there would be slow, romantic music playing on the jukebox. I was totally miserable and mentally had reached rock bottom. Also my phobias had become much worse. I could never sleep without the light on even if there was someone else in the room. On one particular night, I was alone in the room. I took a considerable amount of paracetamol and lay down calmly in bed waiting for bed check. The corporal came in to say good night and asked if I was alright and I said that I was fine, just very tired. I was becoming increasingly drowsy when my friend Maggie called in to say goodnight. She realised that I was not myself and unfortunately or fortunately as the case may be I blurted out what I had done. She immediately called for help and I was whisked away to the sick bay in a flash. I had a rubber tube inserted down my throat to make me vomit and clear out my stomach. Not a pleasant experience. I was put in the sick bay and fell asleep almost immediately as my head hit the pillow. In the cold light of day, I began to realise how silly I had been and what a narrow escape I had had. I was sent to the CO's office the next day… She was quite sympathetic but insisted that I see the medical officer to "talk things through". I was actually warned about him by so many fellow squaddies as apparently he was able to hypnotise people and then molest them in some way, so the rumour went. I was incredibly apprehensive and as the session got under way, I realised that he was actually trying to hypnotise me. I resisted as strongly as I could and after a short while, he brought the session to an end and didn't make me another appointment. I was obviously not a good subject!

Several days later, I felt well enough to go to the Naafi for a drink. Normally, I would leave when the lights were turned down and the slow music started playing knowing what was probably going to happen with those left behind. But on this particular night, I decided to stay and finish my drink.

Lucy was in HQ Company, the block across from mine. She was the same height and build as me with short dark wavy hair. She had beautiful features, was easy to talk to and fancied me like mad. That night she asked me to dance with her which I readily agreed to. This progressed to smooching and kissing and I was quite smitten too. We would meet for our breaks and lunch whenever possible and we really enjoyed each other's company and felt as if we had known each other for years rather than a matter of weeks.

The situation became a little difficult when one of the corporals in my own company started to openly pursue me. However, Lucy and I agreed that one particular night, she would come to my room after bed check. At that time, I had no roommates. Waiting for Lucy to arrive I lay in bed, naked with anticipation, nervous but expectant. Shortly after midnight, Lucy arrived. We barely spoke as she slid under the covers beside me. She was patient and encouraging and I had never experienced such tenderness from a man. Her hands moved deftly over my body as our kisses became more passionate. My whole being tingled and I felt as though I was floating. I hardly knew what was happening to me. It was like nothing I had ever known before.

I knew later that I had experienced my first, and last, for many years, orgasm.

It was very difficult to keep our relationship a secret and shortly after this, Jackie approached me again, this time with a gift of chocolates but also saying she could make it very difficult for my "friend".

However, Lucy and I had decided that when my discharge came through, we would rent a flat in the town centre together.

Faced with what Jackie could do even though I was warned off by one of her colleagues, I was worried that she could make it difficult for Lucy. Meeting was much easier as we were in the same block and she had her own room. It was so easy to spend the night with her and of course her room had a lock so there was no chance of being interrupted. The sex was totally different from my experience with Lucy. She was so different; she was a "receiver" not a giver, incredibly selfish. I did miss Lucy so much although we met occasionally to discuss the situation.

Eventually my discharge came through and it was decided that I should stay with Jackie's friends in London until I found somewhere of my own. They were a gay couple, warm, loving and friendly. I did find a room on the same street but never actually moved in. Jackie's visits became less and less and the excuses more and more plus she was always drinking far too much wherever I did see her.

I travelled into the city every day and did find one job as a telex operator. I also tried my hand at selling encyclopaedias door to door but I was totally useless at the hard sell. I was thoroughly unhappy although I had no longer wished to remain in London with so many mixed memories, given Jackie's philandering, it was with a heavy heart and many misgivings that I once more took a train back to my native Yorkshire.

Chapter 7
Return to Rotherham
and 'Two Mistakes'

My first port of call was to my nanna's where, as always, I received a warm welcome with no recriminations. After a few days of relaxing, helping in the shop and just enjoying her company, Nanna tactfully suggested that I should go home and let my mother know where I was. This led to the inevitable of course. I was told I couldn't live with Nanna but had to go back to the family home. My own bedroom was now occupied by one of my younger sisters. I had to be content with sharing a room with another sister which wasn't actually too bad now that we were older and she worked shifts as a nurse at the local hospital.

With no job or income, I had to sign on the "dole" but after a few weeks, following a visit from an unemployment officer, my benefit was increased as my mother needed "board money". Luckily for me and her, I found a job some weeks later in the finance section at a local engineering firm. At last, I could pay my mother and still have money for a few luxuries and going out instead of having to accept cast offs from my sister although I was extremely grateful for them. I stayed with the engineering company for several months and enjoyed not only the work but all the attention I received from a 99% male workforce! There was one particular chap who for some reason became quite besotted with me even though he was married and old enough to be my father. He would surreptitiously give me gifts of chocolates and sometimes flowers. He even gave me driving lessons but there was never any physical contact. I suppose I just used him, which looking back, wasn't a very nice thing to do.

Several months later, I was able to obtain a position as bookkeeper at The Abbey National Building Society, which is now Santander. I was employed as a bookkeeper but eventually became a cashier and I also dealt with mortgage applications. One day, after accepting an application, after a meeting with a very tall good-looking gentleman, our manager said, 'Do you know who that was?' I hadn't really taken that much notice being busy as usual. 'It was James Fox, the actor,' he said. Apparently he had turned his back on acting for personal reasons but luckily for all his fans and admirers, he eventually went back to it.

At that time, there wasn't an awful lot to do in the town. People tended to gravitate to the "Grapes" pub in Dalton.

It was on one of our "girls" nights out there that I met Jason. He was tall, dark and very handsome and had a good job at the steelworks (it was either Pit or Steel in Rotherham). For weeks, I resisted his attempts to have sex with me but everyone else seemed to be doing it, so why not me? We were in the liberated 70s. But soon I realised that I was pregnant and that I didn't want to spend the rest of my life with Jason. Nor did my mother want that for me and so she organised a termination at the local hospital where she worked. I was only kept in one night but walking home alone the next day, I was actually filled with a feeling of loss—but also relief. During the following week, Jason arrived at my office screaming that I had killed his baby. It was true, but it had been my baby too.

My 21st was not a big event as things go these days. There were five of us! I received a white vanity case from the family; I have no idea what else. I was probably too drunk to remember. We spent the night drinking cheap sherry in the street before travelling to the "penthouse" in Sheffield, returning on the "milk train" early the next morning.

Shortly after, I met Craig. I suppose in a way he was pretty similar to Jason and I fell into yet another futile relationship. I wasn't on the pill and within months, I was pregnant again! This time I tried everything possible to get rid of it but to no avail. I even went to Jason's, home where his father plied me with gin and a steaming hot bath before having sex with me in my drunken stupor!

This time I didn't tell my mother. We went over to Leeds; Craig was totally in agreement to the BPAS. I was told I would have to travel to Liverpool for the termination. It was fortunate that most of the family were away on holiday. Second time around, I suffered pain and severe bleeding which I had to hide from my family until I felt better.

After all this, I felt I needed a holiday so it was with two sisters and two friends who had heard so much about Costa Brava and all the "fellas" that we booked a ten day stay in Lloret de Mar for the summer of '71. I (all of us really) couldn't wait for it to come around. Sun, sea, sangria and sex with a capital S. It was all that the brochure had predicted.

Needless to say, we were all paired-up pretty soon. I decided to change to blonds this time and Gunter (German of course) was my holiday romance even though his English wasn't great, it was certainly better than my German. Long days lying in the sun were followed by even longer nights, drinking, dancing and you've guessed it—having sex. Gunter turned out to be more than a holiday romance and we corresponded when we both returned home. He even arranged to call me at my nanna's house. We didn't have a telephone at that time. However, the distance seems to have been an issue or perhaps the language as the relationship just petered out after a few more weeks.

It was 1971 when computers were the up-and-coming business tool for all forward-looking organisations. The Abbey National had arranged for the area trainer to spend several days at the local branches to teach the rudiments of the system to selected staff.

I was absolutely bowled over when he arrived. He was totally gorgeous and I could barely concentrate on what he had to say. I found out that he was staying in a local hotel (strangely enough, the hotel was knocked down years later and I came to live in one of the flats that was built on its site). That evening on my way to Sheffield for a date with my current man, I plucked up my courage and called the hotel. I was trembling as I waited to be connected, and then a deep sensual voice said, 'Hello.'

'Hi,' I said. It is Angela from work. As you don't know the area, I thought you might like someone to show you around this week.' With fingers, legs and anything else that would cross, I waited for his reply.

'Yes, I'd like that,' he said.

'What about tonight?'

'Sorry, I've got plans for tonight but tomorrow is good.'

We met the following night and every night for that week. Whenever he was in the area, we would meet up and he even came back to Rotherham on two occasions. He was an avid Grimsby supporter and, of course, we had to have an evening at a match even though I never understood football, nor still do for that matter. Later on, I even stayed for a week of my holiday at his parents in Lincolnshire. Being alone in the house several times, we never had sex much to my great disappointment as he was a virgin and I think he was a little afraid as he knew I wasn't. He was incredibly career minded and eventually he said, 'Right girl, wrong time.' So that was that—how long he did expect me to wait while he climbed the career ladder. We did keep in touch for a while. And after I was married, I did visit him in Middleborough when he had received his first big promotion but when he formed a serious relationship, our friendship dwindled as he said she was a very jealous woman. It was in the summer of 1989 that I heard the distressing news that he had been murdered in a car park by his wife's lover. What a terrible waste and total devastation for his parents, brother and children. I did write to his parents and received a lovey letter back as they did remember me as the pretty girl their son had brought to stay.

Chapter 8
Married – Return to Yorkshire

It was August 12, 1972. Having been "stood-up" on a Saturday evening when I was ready to go out I was angry and upset. I was full of thoughts of *How dare he do this to me?* My sister, her boyfriend and a female friend had been invited to a graduation party. I was determined I wasn't staying in the house alone on a Saturday night. Our parents and the rest of the family were away for the weekend at the caravan. After much cajoling, my sister agreed to let me tag along. First stop was the pub along the way of course.

The party was pretty good—a big house plenty to drink, music etc. but for Susan and I, no talent! But at 10:30 pm, all that changed. Small groups of males started to arrive having been to various pubs on the way. I went into the hall and looked towards the kitchen. In the middle of a small group of what could only be described as students was the one I decided I was going home with. He was stocky, ginger-haired with a beard and glasses. Very intellectual, I suspected just what I was looking for after the selection of men I had dated since arriving back in Rotherham. I gathered he was a student at York University. Studying maths and computer science, just about to start his final year. As it happened, he lived locally during the holidays—10 doors away from my maternal grandmother. One of my sisters and I paid him a visit on the way back from our Grandma the following day and that was the beginning of another relationship, but one that was to last for over 30 years! In October Mark went back to university but we tried to meet most weekends either there or in our home town.

It was January 1973. Mark and I had become engaged on the previous Boxing Day as it was the day Mark's parents had married; we had planned our wedding for mid-July what year. It must have been a weekend as I know I didn't have to work. I went downstairs to be met by my mother who was obviously upset and distressed. Upon asking her what was the matter, she told me that she had woken up in the night as she thought she could hear someone moving about downstairs. She had gone downstairs and opened the door to the 'best room' only to find one of my younger siblings having sex on the carpet! Horror of horrors! Although I laugh about it now.

She told my sister that she must marry or leave the house. My sister, being as strong-willed and stubborn as our mother, did both within a matter of weeks.

There was nothing exciting during this courtship. Mark and I got together at weekends, when I wasn't forced to stay at home to help with housework or babysitting, and holidays. I spent one or two weekends at the university but had to tell my mother that I would be staying in one of the guestrooms! We even had a week in the family caravan but even then we had to say that friends would be with us, we couldn't say that we would be alone. Within months, we were engaged and our small celebration was held on Boxing Day, the day Mark's parents had married.

It was shortly after this that I saw my first psychiatrist. By now, I was convinced that someone was trying to kill me. I couldn't stay alone in the house at night and I couldn't sleep if everyone else was sleeping. I was also convinced that I heard noises in the house or someone treading up the stairs if I was in bed. It became so bad that one night I locked myself in the bathroom and shouted and shouted for over an hour before my mother rescued me and let me sleep with my sister.

The psychiatrist was hopeless! After only fifteen minutes, he told me that it was guilt because I believed that I had murdered my father, gave me a prescription and I never saw him again.

Mark was very sympathetic but it was professional help that I needed. By now, I had started to quell my fears with alcohol in the hope that it would help me to sleep and, therefore, not to think.

It was during this time that Mark's mother was diagnosed with cancer. A great shock. The progression was rapid. By March, she was bed-bound but the family (Mark's father and grandparents, as they all lived together) wanted her at home and not in hospital or in a hospice. It was an incredibly stressful time as each day saw her gradually move closer and closer to death. She died in May just six weeks before our planned wedding. Several relatives wanted us to cancel or postpone the wedding but as we both had jobs to go to in Reading, Berkshire, after the wedding, it was deemed impossible. And we both felt that Mark's mother would not have wanted us to do that anyway. I can't remember much about it now, the day seemed so hurried and short, only that my mother insisted that the wedding take place in the morning, so Mark's best man and friends couldn't drink before the wedding ceremony. (Mark's original choice of best man, Graham, was unavailable as he was climbing Mont Blanc at the time.) I do remember Mark kneeling down and exposing the price of his squeaky new shoes to the congregation! My four sisters were bridesmaids and my stepfather gave me away. By this time with the passing of years and more maturity on my part, our relationship had become a good one. The reception was sherry on arrival and a ham salad followed by trifle for 100 guests, which my parents paid for. I paid for the dresses and shoes and accessories (for some bizarre reason I still have my wedding dress.) Mark paid for the church, flowers, taxis and photographs out of his summer holiday jobs. Certainly not the sort of wedding affair one sees nowadays.

We left Rotherham in the late afternoon to begin our "honeymoon". One night in a hotel in Beaconsfield before going on to our new home in Reading. A home, I might add, I had never seen before. Due to time and finances Mark had agreed to view and purchase alone.

The street was a long, Victorian terrace by the side of the Kennet Canal. Not what I was used to but I hoped for better inside. Unfortunately, that was not to be. When the door opened, my heart sank. There were no carpets on the floor and some of the floorboards were in disrepair. We purchased two chairs and a bed from the previous owner along with a small Formica table and two kitchen chairs. The kitchen and bathroom was a "lean-to" on the back of the house. I was devastated that this was to be my new home but being newly married and very much in love, it was something we should have to face together.

We settled into married life well. We both had good jobs. Mark with a computer consultancy and I had transferred from Rotherham with the Abbey National. Money was an issue even with a staff mortgage and being "Northerners" in the South of England then was no joke. "No quiche North of Watford Gap" and "trouble at mill lass". Consequently, we travelled back to Yorkshire every two weeks to see family, as I was terribly homesick, and to fill the car boot with provisions from Asda. It was during our first few months in Reading that we heard on the radio that our friend, Graham, who should have originally been our best man, was lost in Antarctica. His love of the outdoors had led him to apply for and be accepted on the BASS. Apparently, he and two other members of the team had gone climbing having first checked the weather conditions with Cambridge back in England. However, an unexpected storm had blown up and they had been unable to return to camp. The search continued when the storm abated but there was no sign of any of the three of them. A memorial service was held in Rotherham at the church which Graham's parents attended and the church was overflowing. The only consolation for all the mourners was that Graham had died doing what he loved, which is so often the case with lovers of extreme or dangerous sports.

It was also in that year that Nanna became ill. I was told that she was having a routine operation, but not what for, but unfortunately, she didn't recover from it. I was incredibly sad that I hadn't seen her before and mortified that I couldn't even attend the funeral due to work and finances.

Neither of us could settle in the south. I felt completely isolated and my drinking along with my mental health had become a problem. The psychiatrist that I saw said that if I had a job and could study, then I didn't need his help! So 13 months later, when an opportunity to move to Leeds came up, we jumped at the chance.

Incredible as it may seem, for the same price that we sold our "2 up 2 down" in Reading, we were able to purchase a lovely three-bed semi in a sought-after area of Leeds close to Roundhay Park.

I wasn't able to obtain a transfer this time so I took temporary positions. I still had dreams of becoming a primary school teacher and to this end, I applied to James Graham Teacher Training College. Imagine my great delight when shortly after my interview, I was informed that I had been accepted. I was ecstatic! However, the euphoria did not last long. Upon applying for a grant, I was informed that as a married woman, I was not eligible for a grant! We couldn't, therefore, afford for me to stop working and my dreams were once again crushed, not for the first, nor for the last time. I then secured a temporary position with the finance section of the education department and after several months, I was given a permanent position.

Later that year, I was notified that Nanna had left all my father's children a sum of money for which I was so grateful. It meant that we were able to purchase a carpet and suite and settee for the lounge.

Our own new furniture at last instead of second-hand and hand-me-downs.

Chapter 9
Hospitalised

I enjoyed the work with LCC but it was not particularly taxing. In the 70s, local government was overstaffed and under-worked which changed dramatically in the 80s. By this time, I was so neurotic and phobic that I couldn't be in the house alone. Mark and I left together in the mornings and I would wait until he had finished work before I could go home.

I was still dwelling on the death of my father which didn't help matters. To this end, I decided to trace and contact my father's best friend at the time of his death. He had been at university with him and was now a Roman Catholic priest in Bradford, not that many miles from Leeds. I wrote to him and then we had a brief telephone conversation before arranging that he would visit me at home. It was quite wonderful to see him after 16 years and he didn't seem to have changed at all. We exchanged family gossip, as he was one of my younger sister's godfathers. He then became quite serious and told me that the week before my father died, he had wanted to invite him on a trip away but had thought better of it as he had a young family. He was very regretful about not having done so as he believed that it could have prevented what happened. He did attend my father's funeral which my mother said was something he may have had to wrestle with, as it is a cardinal sin in the eyes of the Catholic Church to take one's own life.

This didn't make things much easier, in fact it caused more anguish than I could have imagined, as I just kept going over things in my head over and over again, particularly at night.

In sheer desperation, I made an appointment to see a new GP. He was extremely understanding and sympathetic and referred me to a psychiatrist in Hyde Terrace, Dr Brown, who later immigrated to America. He was probably the only person who actually understood my problems and was able to help to a large extent. The first course of action was to find a suitable medication which, although it helped, made me so docile and sleepy that I often fell asleep at my desk. However, there is never an instant solution in the case of mental issues/problems.

A few weeks later, it was decided that I should be admitted to the psychiatric ward of Leeds Infirmary. Unfortunately, it was a ward that catered for "women's surgical" as well. The stigma attached to anyone suffering from mental disorders was truly diabolical. During communal meal times when the conversation got around to why people were there, I used to reply, 'Just for observation.' The response was, 'You're not a nutter or looney then.' Eventually though, it became very difficult to hide and the reaction was as expected. Other patients gave me a wide berth except for the other "nutters".

My stay lasted six weeks and during that time, Mark visited twice a day, before and after work. My mother came once! Rotherham to Leeds was like asking her to climb Mount

Everest particularly when she was informed that a lot of my problems stemmed from childhood.

The highlight of the week was a visit from the now infamous Jimmy Saville who volunteered as a hospital porter on Tuesdays. He sat on my bed, as he did many others, and gave me several autographs. I saw him many times over the years in and about Leeds and was even photographed with him along with my granddaughter, but had no idea what was to "come out" about him so many years later!

Upon being discharged, I was given behavioural therapy which was going quite well until several months later, I realised that I was pregnant. Horror of horrors! I couldn't even take responsibility for myself let alone a baby. And there was also the financial aspect of it. My medical teams were only too happy to sanction a termination under the circumstances. I felt no sadness after the event—just enormous relief. I'm sure this will shock some people but you have to experience a situation before passing judgments on others. I feel it's a bit like being homophobic or racist. All members of a community have different views and needs.

My mental health steadily improved over the next few months and years and I was actually able to come home from work and stay in an empty house alone. It was an immense struggle but I made it. From Mark's point of view, things were not going quite so well. He had become increasingly unhappy with the company he had transferred to Leeds with. There were certain "cliques" of which he wasn't a part and many members of staff were being paid far beyond their capabilities. So when he was offered the position of IT manager at one of the client's sites, he jumped at the chance. It was more responsibility but it was also more challenging and more money! However, he had always dreamed of starting his own business and started to do some freelance work. We also augmented our salaries by delivering envelopes for the electoral register and I would also take part in the election voting process.

I had won several items by entering numerous competitions as I was a regular subscriber to "competitors weekly". We had sold a bicycle, and a few other items which we were able to sell but money was still very tight. We decided to sell my wedding dress and advertised it locally. A few days later a Chinese couple arrived and said that they were interested in buying the dress. They told us that they had taken English names since arriving in Leeds and that they were called Stephen and Suzanna. Stephen was a student at Leeds University studying accountancy. I took Suzanna upstairs to try on the wedding dress. I noticed that she was wearing a gold wedding band.; When I mentioned it, she told me that she and Stephen had been married in the local registry office but that they both wanted photos in wedding attire to send to their parents in Hong Kong. She tried on the dress and it was perfect. However, we decided to let her borrow it rather than buy it; and they agreed to return it the following day after taking photos with friends. Next day, we waited several hours and decided that they had just taken the dress but several minutes later, they arrived with the said wedding dress and a gorgeous box of chocolates. They came in the house and we drank tea and chatted. Mark and Stephen arranged to play squash together the following week. Over several weeks, it became a regular thing and we also went out for Chinese meals together.

One day, we took them home to collect something from their flat. Flat is not the correct word for their home. It was an attic room at the top of an old house in a very bad area of the city. Immediately, we told them to pack their few belongings and move in with us.

They stayed for three months until they found a suitable flat fairly nearby. The sad thing was that they left us on Christmas Day.

Having had a slight altercation with his boss over the fact that one of the shift leaders, who was an immigrant, earned less money than his English equivalent, Mark decided that it was high time to move on. On the strength of a contract from a local agricultural bank, he resigned, installed a computer in the single bedroom and registered a business. He actually went into partnership with one of his old colleagues and so it all started.

Things went very well and after only a few weeks, the business acquired rented accommodation in nearby Dewsbury and "stole" yet another ex-colleague plus employing a secretary and a junior programmer. Eventually, the order book started to fill up and with very prestigious clients too.

Chapter 10
Birth of My Son

In the summer of '78. Mark decided that after four years, it was time to "move on". The business was beginning to make reasonable profits and he wanted a bigger mortgage for tax purposes. We exchanged our homely semi for what can only be described as a "modern box", just over three miles away. It had a decent garden and was easy to manage but you could almost touch the neighbours' walls from the dining room window.

Life plodded on. The business had acquired rented accommodation in Dewsbury and I received a promotion by changing departments with the council. I began to take an ONC in business studies on a day release which I really enjoyed.

It was during this time that I made the acquaintance of Harriet and her husband, Eric. We were to become great friends.

The business thrived and it was able to finance an annual dinner dance weekend away at various hotels in different locations each year.

We had foreign holidays, changed the car three times, ate out often and generally had a very comfortable existence.

But in 1980, after seven years of marriage, I realised that I was pregnant. Horror of Horrors! I was still studying and I wanted a career. Nevertheless, I put my reservations aside and decided to get on with being pregnant "and" violently sick for almost six months. We decided to take an early holiday in Jersey but after the dreadful crossing, which did nothing for my morning sickness, I began to bleed and have a disgusting discharge. We hastened back to Leeds to the hospital where I was told to rest but that I would probably lose the baby!

After a couple of weeks, everything seemed to have settled down despite the reservations and I continued to work until mid-October. After that, the time was spent preparing a room for the imminent arrival and longing to be able to eat without feeling sick again.

On Christmas Eve 1980, we had gone to bed relatively early to be fresh for the next day. However, at 12:50, our burglar alarm set off and I flew out of bed catching my huge stomach on the corner of the bedside cabinet. It was a false alarm so after a cup of tea, we went back to bed. Next morning, I started preparing lunch but felt very unwell and had stomach cramps. I called my mother who said it appeared that I had gone into labour. I called the hospital and they advised me to stay at home as long as possible! By 3:30, I was literally crawling on the floor, grabbing at the furniture. I told Mark that I must go to the hospital 'now'! To which he replied, 'Just let me make some sandwiches, I won't get any dinner.' Some things never change!

By the time my gorgeous baby boy was born at 7:30 pm on Christmas Day, I still only weighed nine and a half stone. Those were the days! Unfortunately, he was jaundiced and was taken away to an incubator where we had to wear gowns and masks to visit him for several days. My mother and stepfather came by to visit the following day which I was so pleased about. We spent the rest of Christmas and New Year in hospital, returning home 10 days later.

I was not a confident mother, as my health visitor kept telling me. I was nervous when he cried and when I had to bathe him but I loved just watching him and realised how wonderful the gift of life was. My son completely changed my outlook on life, I absolutely adored him. The first few weeks were pretty hectic. The health visitor classed me as a "non-confident" parent and came every day for 28 days!

I did get better but after seven years of marriage becoming pregnant had been a shock under the circumstances (for that read *Still Alive*).

In March 1981, one of my lecturers from the polytechnic called to ask if I would be returning to finish my course. Mark had said that he didn't want me to go back to work but I felt as though I was turning into a vegetable at home even though I loved Sam dearly. Consequently, I completed and passed my A.A.T course even with breaks off, when some students actually failed.

A feather in my cap!

In June of that year, we decided to return to Jersey for the holiday that was cut so short the previous year. The hotel was superb and the weather wonderful and my precious little son was a model baby. Upon our return, we employed a nanny in order for me to return to work and also because of the fact that we would still have half my wage which was very important at that time. I had also acquired a bright yellow Ford Fiesta, of which I was very proud, to enable Sam and I to have little outings as well as transport to and from work.

The only major incident that occurred during that time was that Sam had a febrile convulsion. We had just come back from our trip to the shops and I was about to take off his outdoor clothes when suddenly his eyes began to roll and he appeared to be foaming at the mouth and his lips were blue. I panicked, I truly believed that he was having a heart attack, never having had experienced anything of the like before. I dragged him across the floor to the telephone and dialled 999. I then called my neighbour and Mark, who was away on a business trip. The ambulance was incredibly quick and we pelted down Roundhay Road with the blue light flashing and the siren blaring out. Sam had never uttered a syllable or showed any sign of recognition about anything and didn't for at least another four hours. His temperature was sky high and he was sponged down and given medication before being transferred to a children's ward where he and I remained for several days under observation with Mark taking over when I needed a shower or something to eat. It was a terrifying experience as I'm sure any parent will appreciate and one which I wouldn't like to go through again. But some years later, an even more dreadful fate awaited!

The next few years passed relatively smoothly. We had a nanny for Sam which enabled us to use my salary for foreign holidays. Mark's business was becoming quite successful too. He even spent time in Australia making computers there "talk" to computers in England. These along with several achievements were duly recorded in local newspapers. I had my stepfather and sister to take shifts with me during that time, as I was still not confident enough to stay alone. The only disappointments were my three miscarriages in the following three consecutive years. The first was when Sam was 18 months old. I was 12 weeks pregnant. I was coming downstairs in a long, tartan dressing (how could I ever forget what I was wearing?) and I slipped from the third step from the top and bumped all the way dawn to the bottom. At first, I only felt shaken but after several hours, I realised that I was spotting blood. I was admitted to hospital where after a scan and an examination, it was determined that the baby hadn't survived the fall. I then had to undergo surgery to extract the dead foetus. We were terribly disappointed but at that stage knew there would be time hopefully for more children later on. However, the following year, I suffered yet another miscarriage and my disappointment increased along with the thought that I would never have another child as in the past when I had been pregnant I had terminated God's gift of life!

By 1984, Mark felt it was time to move to a bigger home in a better area which we did. My mother and stepfather were horrified when they saw it. "How can you afford this big place" was their reaction. Nonetheless in July 1984, we moved into what was to become a very happy family home for the next 12 years. Strangely enough, the following month, Mark's business moved from Dewsbury into a beautiful Georgian property on the outskirts of Leeds. It was a very successful time all ways round.

On our first day in our new home, the doorbell rang and I opened the door to find a very smart, older woman brandishing a huge bunch of colourful, wonderfully smelling sweet peas. She introduced herself as Muriel Clues from next door and wanted to welcome us to the neighbourhood. After a few weeks of settling in, we invited Muriel and her husband, Arthur, to dinner only to discover that he was The Arthur Clues, international rugby player! He was a complete scream.

He had never lost his Australian accent and the tales he could tell had every one collapsing around the dinner table. Shortly afterwards, he and Muriel moved to a nearby flat as his legs were just not what they used to be. We still got together occasionally until some years later he died. His send-off was a very large affair with many well-known names from the sporting arena in attendance.

Chapter 11
The Birth of My Daughter

In January 1985, I realised I was pregnant yet again. Not wanting to lose yet another baby, we were recommended to see a private consultant. After 14 weeks of hormone injections, it seemed as though the worst was past. However, I continued to put on weight at an increasing pace and by the time Rachel was born in November, I had increased by five stones! I was also on bed rest for several weeks, which and apart from a nanny, we now had a cleaner too. This was a much more difficult birth than Sam and I was induced. I had an epidural this time and couldn't feel a thing, fortunately as the labour seemed to go on forever. But it was worth it when I saw my beautiful daughter, even though I had wanted another boy so that I could make use of all Sam's clothes! (Still Rachel was quite a tomboy and some of the things rather suited her.) We were allowed home after only three days this time.

This time, I was a much more confident parent but I also had help. However, after 8 weeks I missed working so it was agreed that I would help in the accountants' department at Mark's business which was growing in leaps and bounds. A contract with American Express meant that we were guests at

Wimbledon. What an experience! I immediately fell in love with the place and went each year for many years later as will be seen and met so many stars and tennis legends. In 1986, we were staying at the Holiday Inn in Cardiff, as Mark had been working in the city for some clients and felt we would like to visit. On the Saturday morning, as we were wandering around the town centre, we came Sophie Corbett; the daughter of the Ronnie with the glasses. She was promoting "Poppy day" (Remembrance Day) with Simon Weston, the Falklands veteran. We asked if we could have a photograph taken with Sam to which she agreed. The next morning, a photo of Sophie and Sam was in a prominent position on the front page of Cardiff newspaper (Not the last time Sam was to have his name in print!).

We revisited Cardiff several times if only for the "riverside" Chinese restaurant and even spent a rather wonderful Christmas there.

It was during that time that we also visited Glasgow, staying at the Holiday Inn. Imagine our surprise when going up to our room in the lift we came face to face with none other than Billy Connolly who told us that he was in Glasgow to visit his children.

We had many short breaks and occasional holidays in Britain due to the fact that I had always had an incredible and illogical fear of flying but our holiday to Marbellalaga sealed it almost forever.

We were flying from Heathrow to Malaga for a family holiday in August '88: the four of us and a young family friend who was to help with the children. We had just been served our meal and drinks on the BA flight when suddenly the plane began to judder and there was a loud crack in the cabin. Seconds later, we were plummeting earthwards with the oxygen masks dangling in front of our faces and the pre-recorded messages resounding in our ears. "There is no cause for alarm, put the mask over your mouth and nose and breathe normally". The children and our friend were across the aisle from us and Rachel was too small to reach her mask. As the plane was at a sloping angle by now, a stewardess literally crawled up from the front of the plane and handed a small oxygen mask to our friend for Rachel. I truly believed that we were going to die! After what seemed like an eternity, I could see the sea below us and the plane appeared to level out. Almost immediately, there came the voice of the captain over the PA system. 'This is Captain Hill speaking (I will never forget his name). We had a slight problem with the air conditioning system and had to drop from 34,000ft to 10,000 ft. We are returning to Heathrow but we will serve you all complimentary drinks.' By this time, there was panic in the cabin, babies crying, children screaming, parents shouting.

Upon arrival back at Heathrow, we were ushered into a private area and medical assistance was called for to attend to some of the passengers. A BA representative then came to deliver us the information that a plane was being sent from Cardiff as a replacement but would take several hours. We were told that if we didn't take this flight, we would not receive compensation or another flight as Captain Hill had not declared the situation as an airborne emergency. Good heavens, what needs to happen I thought! Many passengers wanted to retrieve their luggage and cancel their trip but eventually most were (including me!) pacified and we waited almost seven hours for our replacement plane. When we did eventually land in Malaga at 2 am, our car hire had been given away!

Later that year saw Sam's second stay in hospital but this time, it was much more serious. He had begun vomiting and complained of a severe headache and was unable to look at light. Immediately, alarm bells rang and I called the doctor who was not our usual GP. Despite my feeling that things were very serious, he left saying that we should keep him cool and wait a little longer. A little while later, I was in real panic. The doctor returned and straight away called an ambulance. The second time Sam had literally flown down Roundhay Road with the blue light flashing and sirens blaring. It was of course meningism but we were very fortunate unlike some families, who have my heartfelt sympathy. Sam was admitted to the children's ward where we stayed for several days whilst he received treatment. Fortunately for us as a family, he recovered with no ill effects.

It was also in that year that we purchased a holiday flat on the east coast. It was in great need of renovation but it seemed like quite an adventure so we put up with the discomfort of the freezing cold bathroom and the damp in one or the bedrooms. We did eventually refurbish the kitchen and bathroom but by that time, the business needed so much time that we sold it in order to move on to better things.

Chapter 12
On the Up and Up – 1

By now, the company was really buzzing and Mark made sure we enjoyed it. Our premises were in the process of being extended. We had our first visit to Disneyland in Florida; this was a special treat for Sam as he had been awarded an academic scholarship at his school. We were taking more and more foreign holidays and had our first Rolls Royce as well as my car. Normally, for at least one of the issues to deal with, appropriate members of staff and their families would join us in such locations as the Canary Islands, Majorca, Cyprus or Sardinia. While the staff worked all day, the families were free to enjoy the sea, sun and sand. In the evenings, we would all eat together. This continued for many years.

The other "perk" which was always looked forward to by all was the annual conferences which had by now become a full weekend. The conference was scheduled for two hours on the Saturday morning but the rest of the weekend was certainly fun-packed with something for everyone from children's entertainers, quizzes, go-karting, hot air ballooning and, of course, the Saturday evening celebrities. We were lucky enough to "capture" such celebs as Sharon Davies, Derek Redmond, Cannon and Ball, Tom O'Connor, Sue

Johnston, Gwen Taylor and the late Emlyn Hughes over the years.

Some years later, however, I learned that one of the children's entertainers had been found guilty of indecent assault on a 14-year-old. He pleaded his innocence but was sentenced to prison. He wrote to me and I agreed to visit him on several occasions in Doncaster Prison. I even employed him again sometime later but horror of horrors! He was accused again of the same offense and pleaded guilty to numerous similar offenses! And I thought I was a good judge of character!

In 1989, we were planning the event at the St Nicholas Hotel in January 1990. I really needed something special to wear to the formal dinner on Saturday night. I tramped the whole of Leeds but to no avail when several people suggested Harrogate. After trying numerous shops which we had been recommended but with no success and just as we were to give up, I noticed what I thought was a spectacular dress on a model in the window of a small obviously exclusive shop. It was the start of a relationship, not only with the shop but also with the young lady who attended to us on that day. My dress had to be made in the size and it cost what can only be described as "an arm and a leg"; it was truly worth it and I did wear it again some later on board the QE2.

The following year, I returned for yet another "creation" and the practice continued over the next few years.

In between of course, with our newfound wealth, I was able to furnish my whole wardrobe from the same establishment. It included many by top designers and I was particularly taken with by Zandra Rhodes. I purchased several of her outfits over a period of time which I still possess. I was also fortunate enough, along with my daughter, to be invited to a lunch with Zandra (although I forget the actual date), along with some other select clients. Rachel had a photo taken with Zandra but I think I missed out.

During the next few years, things from a financial point of view just got better and better. After a disastrous three-day stay in a holiday village in France, we decided that we had had enough! The pool was unusable as it was covered with dead flies and winged creatures of all sorts, women shopped topless in the little supermarket. The French kept all manner of pets on the adjoining balconies and the whole of the walkways and grassed areas had to be avoided due to the enormous amounts of dog poop! Apart from the fact that only one person could fit in the bathroom at a time and when sitting down on the loo your knees touched the door!

Through American Express, we travelled south and found the Hotel du Palais in Biarritz, supposedly where Edward and Mrs Simpson consummated their relationship, or so we were told. However, despite the wonderful hotel and picturesque town, the weather was appalling and we moved yet further south into Spain. We hit upon, via Amex again, a marvellous hotel on the Spanish coast just south of Barcelona, in a place called S'Agaro, a very unspoilt part of the coast-line, or at least it was. The hotel "Hostal de la Gavina" was truly a breath of fresh air and we took our holidays there for the following two years.

It was on our second visit to "La Gavina" that we first made the acquaintance of Eusebio Sacristan and his new wife. The local tennis coach had arranged a partner for. Mark. When he returned to the hotel, he proudly announced that he had played tennis with, and beaten, the captain of Barcelona and Spanish football! We learnt that he and his wife were actually on their honeymoon. They had married in Spain and flown to Florida for their post-wedding holiday. Unfortunately, the crowds and the inability to communicate in English had spoiled their visit and they had returned to S'Agaro to complete their holiday in Spanish luxury. And so a friendship began that was to last several years. We were invited as Eusebio's guests to "Nous Camp" to watch Barcelona beat Zaragoza in the King's Cup. When Barcelona played Manchester United at Old Trafford, we stayed at the same hotel as the team as well as being invited to the match.

We met several times in Spain over the coming years. Both Eusebio and his wife learnt to speak some English which was useful as our combined Spanish, at that time, wasn't wonderful. During that time, they had two beautiful children, a boy and a girl.

On our third trip to S'Agaro, we found out that the tennis coach owned a small tennis club in Playa D'aro just a few miles from the hotel. We became regulars there over the years and joined in its many weekly tournaments.

We also made several good friends whom we met every year, some even visiting us in England.

It was on that trip that we decided that we would like to buy an apartment there. So early the following year, Mark and Sam went over to Spain to view an apartment which was for sale very close to the tennis club. It was perfect as it was a real Spanish not the type that foreigners normally buy as a holiday home. That summer, we had enough spare furniture shipped over to complete our very own Spanish "home". We also bought a small speedboat which we kept on an adjoining beach.

Apart from the summers, we would spend most school holidays and half-terms there too. We had our favourite restaurants, bars and cafes but we still used the "Gavina" for its pool and its wonderful dining facilities.

In addition to the wonderful hotels, which we able to stay in, I believe that if you are able, and obviously have the means to do so, there are three journeys that are a must. A flight on Concorde, a voyage on the QE2 and a rail journey on the Orient Express. Unfortunately, due to my sheer terror of flying (I didn't fly for over four years but travelled to Spain and rest of Europe by rail or car). I have never experienced Concorde. That was left to Sam and Mark who experienced a champagne flight from England to France and back again. However, as a family, we did spend time on the QE2 in 1991. It will always remind me of the blockbuster film *Titanic*. The sheer opulence of it all. We had staterooms with a sea view, which in hindsight was a mistake for me. Had it not been an enormous floating hotel, I think I would have enjoyed it much more. I found it difficult to find my way around and after the emergency drill, was in constant fear that we would have to put it into action. This having been said, The QE2 was a magnificent vessel. There were endless quantities of gourmet food 24 hours a day. Dinner on board was quite spectacular and all the guests dressed accordingly. There was every form of entertainment one could wish for: cinema, theatre, casino, deck games, quizzes etc., apart from the pools and the gym. There was not really any time to enjoy the luxury of the stateroom!

The "Orient Express" was a much calmer travelling experience for myself which I enjoyed in 1994. It was only a short trip through Yorkshire one evening with a superb dinner on board but it was enough to whet one's appetite for a much longer journey through Europe.

Apart from journeys there are certainly a number of hotels that warrant a visit. One of these is the George V in Paris. We were lucky enough to spend several days there in 1996 breaking our journey to Spain. It is, or was, total luxury personified. The elegant period decor throughout the hotel is magnificent and the whole hotel actually breathes wealth and opulence as soon as you step inside once you're Rolls Royce has been parked for you of course. The bathrooms are incredible, with an abundance of leading brands of toiletries, and you can bury yourself in the thick, soft pile of the towels and bathrobes. You can just imagine yourself as Cleopatra in the huge bath, minus the milk of course!

I have fond memories of that stay and beautiful photos of Rachel and I looking elegant and very befitting for dinner in the grand dining room. Fond memories tinged with a certain amount of sadness that those times can never be recaptured.

Chapter 13
On the Up and Up – 2

One of Mark's efforts at climbing the social ladder was to "groom" our local MP (on whom I understand Rick Mayall based one of his most famous characters).

The promise of finance and the use of telephones during his election campaigns led us to being invited to lunch on the terrace at the Houses of Parliament. It was one of my many memorable experiences. We were given the "grand tour" before lunching outdoors overlooking the Thames. The setting was perfect, the food exquisite and the people spotting excellent. We were also invited to the said MP's beautiful Yorkshire home for a dinner party and met his extremely amiable and talented wife as well as several other well-known friends. The acquaintance continued for several years.

It was 1984 that I first met Matthew Corbett (David I believe) and Sooty. Sam and I went to a performance at the Cottage Road cinema in Headingly. Almost at the end of the show, Matthew Corbett said there would be various gifts for the first woman to run up on stage and give him a kiss. Naturally, I wanted to get all the goodies for Sam so I left him sitting there and charged onto the stage hoping to avoid the crowds. But as I kissed Matthew on the cheek, I realised I was the only other person on stage—except for the puppets of course! We chatted for a while and I was duly given various gifts items for Sam and then shown off backstage.

So when I was organising Mark's 40th birthday bash in June of '92, I decided that I needed special entertainment for the hordes of children that would be there. So who did I think of? Matthew of course and Sooty. Particularly given that it was Sooty's 40th birthday too.

My PA (as I was now head of the human resources department) somehow managed to find a telephone number for Mathew and after some discussion, although he was most surprised at the request, we agreed a fee and the deal was sealed.

Apart from Matthew and Sooty, we had a dog entertainer, a skydiver making an entrance with a box of "milk tray" and numerous other activities apart from mountains of food, drink and cake; I still remember what we were both wearing (without photos). It was actually a very happy day.

Thereafter, whenever Matthew and Sooty were performing, we were able to speak to him after the show and on two separate occasions, Sam was invited on stage to participate. By this time, our financial situation had become better and better. We had several Rolls Royces and a BMW. The business was thriving and both children were in private schools. Unfortunately, Sam was actually in boarding school in the next county as his previous prep school had been unable to deal with his strange artistic and at times, his somewhat bizarre behaviour. The company was thriving and by now, I had a PA and several other members of staff in our ever-growing human resources department.

We continued to spend our summers in Spain and exchanged our speedboat for a two-berth boat, a jet ski and a jeep! We even employed a skipper. We were certainly on the "up and up".

It was on one of our visits to London that Rachel and I met Lennie Henry and his daughter. We had gone to a matinee at the Savoy Theatre and had just taken our seats when I was distracted by a very familiar voice behind us. I didn't need to turn round to see who it was; I would have recognised that voice anywhere. But I did turn around and said hello to him. We exchanged a few words about daughters, sweets and the imminent performance and of course, he gave us an autograph. What a lovely man. I didn't turn round again, I suppose he gets harassed enough and when all is said and done, he needs his privacy to enjoy being a parent. On one of our other many visits to London, it was to see David Copperfield. For some reason, Mark had decided to stay at the Milestone Hotel in Kensington. Imagine our surprise when we found out the following morning that David, along with his mother, were guests of the hotel too. Although we were not able to meet him personally, we did chat with his mother and she very kindly obtained a signed program for us.

Two other visits to London to the Albert Hall were to see The Cirque du Soleil (What a small world Sam is now a friend of the Las Vegas manager of the group) and my very favourite Joaquin Cortez.

By now, the business was totally exploding. We had the property extended and won a prestigious award for the decoration of the interior which I had supervised along with one the contractors. The ceilings were returned to their former glory and I went to London to receive the award which was a very gratifying and unique experience. Shortly after that, the business was nominated for another award and we were lucky enough to be shortlisted. The event was wonderful with the winner to be announced by Lord King himself. I was even luckier to be seated next to him at dinner and to actually be called 'young lady' by him. I suppose it's all relative really! We didn't win that award though; it went to a pig farmer. Well, food is more important than computers in Yorkshire! I believe it was about this time that we became subscribers to The Prince's Trust, a very worthy cause in itself, but a spin-off was that we got to attend various film premiers and also to obtain attendance at the wonderful BAFTA Awards. At a Prince' Trust event, which Sam and I attended, he was lucky enough to be seated next to "Q" of the 007 film fame. A very interesting individual although I didn't get a word in edgeways! We attended many events of this kind over the coming years which always meant a trip to Harrogate and a new frock!

It was in January 1994 that my maternal grandmother reached the majestic age of 100. The nursing home arranged a tea party and the family arranged a visit from the local mayor. By this time, however, any lovely grandmother could neither see nor hear properly and was quite confused at times. It was explained to her that she had received a framed telegram from the queen, depicting Windsor Castle but I'm not sure that she fully comprehended. There was a beautiful photo in the local paper consisting of four generations.

Chapter 14
Rubbing Shoulders – 1

I have always been a great tennis fan, although a mediocre player, since the days when my next-door neighbour and I played in Clifton Park, pretending to be Angela Mortimer and Christine Trueman. However, I'm not sure who ever won as we spent most of the time picking up the balls! I was there in jubilee year cheering on my heroine, Virginia, in her victory over Betty Stove. That year I managed to photograph the Queen through the car window when she visited Leeds. Little did I know then that I would see her again in the flesh at Buckingham Palace many years later.

Imagine my delight, when years later, Mark saw in some publication or other that Virginia Wade herself would be hosting a tennis forum at Gleneagles in Scotland. At the time, all the families were members of the local tennis club and it was felt that we should try to be part of the event. No sooner said than done! Money can pave the way to most things.

It was our first venture across the border as a family although I had previously had a day-away trip to Edinburgh. Of course, we arrived in the Rolls Royce to be given the Gleneagles very special treatment.

Our welcome dinner was the group's opportunity to meet my tennis heroine. I was a complete bag of nerves and actually wanted to back out of the evening as I had done on many occasions, citing my nervous condition. It always came in handy. But this time it didn't work.

We were all presented to Virginia in turn before the welcome dinner but nerves get the better of me and I turned into a red-raced jabbering idiot. In subsequent years, I fared much better and was not only able to hold a conversation with Virginia but even benefited from her tennis coaching. The association led to us being able to get in touch with her on our frequent visits to Wimbledon and watch her graceful figure in veteran's matches.

I have still followed her many commentaries on TV being unable now to attend that great British event, Wimbledon. Champagne, strawberries and mingling with stars of screen and stage.

Everyone has screen idols. These days its Brad Pitt, Leonardo di Caprio, etc. Mine in this order were Dirk Bogarde, Kenneth Brannah and Sean Bean.

Apart from being avid tennis fans, Sam and I were theatre buffs. Our attraction had grown, when in 1992, Sam had a part in Sheridan's "The Rivals" at the Leeds Playhouse. It was during those few weeks that one of the actors took Sam under his wing. This led to, on our next visit to Stratford, being given a guided tour of the 'Swan' theatre when he was performing there. Also in that cast was David Harewood who has certainly gone on from strength to strength since then. Sometime later, we were privileged to be in the audience for Kenneth Brannagh's rendition of "Hamlet". It was impossible to meet him but having written a note of thanks and appreciation some weeks later, I received an autographed copy of the wonderful silver and white programme.

My experience with, some years later, (well not actually with) Sean Bean, a fellow neighbour from Sheffield, was somewhat less than satisfactory. Having waited for almost an hour at the stage door, I was told that he wouldn't come out or even give an autograph. Cunning was called for! I found the nearest wine shop, bought a decent bottle of red wine and "bribed" one of the theatre staff to get an autograph. He duly went away and returned with the said Monika, whether it was authentic I never knew!

My adoration for my screen idol Dirk Bogarde was long and intense. For years I had his photograph on my bedside cabinet. My favourite films, which I have watched so many times, were "The Servant" (with a wonderful Yorkshire accent) "The Victim" and "Accident".

I watched many others of course but these were the ones to see over and over again in which I believe he showed his true genius.

In his later years, D.B began to publish his memoirs. I soaked up every written word with true relish.

I was justly rewarded when he spoke at the Leeds Playhouse and I was actually able to ask him a question. He signed a copy of his latest recollections which unfortunately I was forced to sell with so many of my prized possessions some years later.

All prime ministers (or at least most) have been known to write memoirs and publish books, Margaret Thatcher was no exception.

A chance to meet the "Iron Lady", if only at a booking signing was too good an opportunity to miss. Consequently, I travelled to London with Mark, a work colleague and Rachel to join a huge line of followers to obtain a signature and at least a word from the first female prime minister. Knowing that Mrs Thatcher's daughter-in-law was from Texas, I duly purchased a bunch of yellow roses from a street vendor and waited in line with Rachel.

As predicted, Mrs Thatcher signed my book and having taken the roses from Rachel, said, 'How appropriate my daughter-in-law is from Texas.'

Well done me!

A great favourite of both mine and as always been Hugh Laurie. He had just published his first novel, a detective spoof which he was to read from at Waterstones. Sam and I managed to secure front row seats and spoke to him during the book signing. It would be impossible to get so close to him now that he's such a big star in America so that was another one for the memory box.

Apart from being an enjoyable time, that time was also a particularly scary one. I was at home with Rachel who had a home visit from the chiropodist (several verrucas—no doubt from the swimming pool!). The telephone rang and I picked up almost straight away expecting it to be Mark. However, a male voice at the other end said, 'I know where you are and I'm going to kill you.' I was frozen to the spot. I put the phone down but it rang again with the same caller and the same message. Slamming down the receiver, I called Mark who sent someone from the office to stay until he came home from work. We didn't call the police that day as the world is full of crank callers. A couple of days later, when I was alone, it happened again and again. This time we did call the police. Luckily, we were due to go away for a few days and I was immensely relieved. Whilst we were away, the person called again and our cleaner answered it but he got short shrift from her! It wasn't until a few months later that we learned that a man, who worked on a local telephone exchange, had been charged with 56 counts of making threatening phone calls. It goes to show you can't always trust people in a position of confidentiality.

Chapter 15
Rubbing Shoulders – 2

The relationship between Mark and our MP flourished. We were invited to dine at his beautiful house in Yorkshire and subsequently received our invitation to a Royal Garden Party at Buckingham Palace in the summer of 1996. Yet another memory and photo for the album—new hat of course. The security was intense as one would expect and the setting was something that I could never have imagined. One only sees the front of Buckingham Palace on TV, in films and on postcards but behind the magnificent facade are extensive gardens, grounds and the famous orangery.

There were minor royals, dignitaries, MPs, representatives from numerous charity organisations and branches of the armed forces, and, like us, ordinary members of the public. Food and drink were plentiful, and I imagine expensive.

We had a long wait for her Majesty—aching feet, sweating head in the new hat—but it was worth it. She arrived accompanied by Prince Philip, looking regal, cool and elegant in lemon and white. She traversed the middle of the waiting admirers stopping briefly to chat to members of the various charities, armed forces and anyone who took her interest, some were wearing fancy dress! She stayed for at least an hour, re-entering the back doors of her London residence.

For me she is, has been, and always will be the perfect monarch. The only blot on her copybook, for me anyway, being the way she handled the tragic death of Princess Diana. Not only the people's princess but an inspiration too many throughout the world.

Wimbledon had been one of our favourite events since Mark and I were the first guests of clients America Express. Sometimes we were able to obtain tickets via the general draw but normally from our tennis club draw. This year was no different. The only difference was that due to our tennis sponsoring and two Spanish tennis friends, we were able to secure Mark's work experience of a lifetime—supposedly carrying bags for the Aranatxa Sanchez. With our passes, this secured Mark and I an entrance into all areas of the AELTC except the dressing rooms.

We ate in the players' dining room, watched all the matches we wanted to and Sam had the time of his life chatting to players, both past and future champions. We stayed in a hotel nearby for the whole two weeks which was perfect.

The fortnight was rounded off by attending the men's final between Richard Krajicek and Pete Sampras. Richard won and to our astonishment not only did he not disappear but made straight for his players' lounge. Obviously, we followed only to be invited to toast the champion in champagne with his small entourage! What an experience for two avid tennis fans!

I believe it was that year too that Sam and I "bumped into" Martin Clunes and John Morrisey of "Men behaving badly" fame. Sam, who was by then very proficient with his hobby of magic, entertained them to a few tricks.

Over the years, we also met the Jensen's, Goran Ivanišević, Tim Henman, André Aggassi. Lindsay Davenport to name but a few!

We rounded off that year with Sam's 16th birthday in New York with our two friends whom we had flown over from Spain as a surprise (Sadly they too are no longer together). We stayed in the magnificent Plaza Hotel for a week which was truly amazing and our first visit to New York. Obviously we did all the usual tourist sights Times Square, Empire State Building, Statue of Liberty, Rockefeller Squares and tried the open-air ice-skating there). We hit the shops on 5th Avenue and Rachel hit F A Schwartz toy shop with a vengeance! On Christmas Eve, we were in Planet Hollywood, celebrating M's birthday but had to wait until the clock struck midnight for the cake and the true celebrations. My Christmas Day boy. On Christmas Day, we went to the Radio Show, apparently a tradition in New York. In the late afternoon, we sampled the Christmas brunch buffet. It was no ordinary buffet I can tell you. There were ice statues everywhere not only for decoration but to keep the enormous amount of seafood fresh. There was every imaginable type of food you could think of. I believe we spent at least three hours enjoying not only the food, drink, but the sheer experience of it all. After a hectic week, we flew down to Florida for the New Year.

Goodbye 1996 and Hello 1997!

The New Year brought with it problems for me personally. It didn't matter that I had a wonderful job, a lovely home etc., my mental problems just would not go away. A neighbour who was a medical person recommended an excellent psychiatrist whom I began to see. Apart from all my phobias, I also had to contend with, as I had done for years, the perpetual browbeating and belittling by Mark. Members of my family have asked me several times why I put up with it. It aggravated my mental state and on two occasions led to attempted suicides. I don't believe these were ever serious attempts as I never took enough tablets to do long term damage; it was a cry for help. Mark was present at two of the sessions over a period of time but refused to take any responsibility or to compromise on anything so he stopped attending and then decided that the sessions weren't doing me any good!

Chapter 16
We Are Millionaires –
1 April 1998

The past few years of trying to keep the company afloat, and a viable proposition for a buyer, had finally paid off and the end of the rainbow was in sight. The previous months had been spent in negotiating the sale of our third "child". It was touch-and-go for several weeks with due diligence and trying to maintain as much secrecy as possible. There were clandestine meetings in Leeds, London and Oxford. Price was obviously an issue. The buyer was a shrewd businessman and although Mark was a formidable opponent in most situations, I believe Robert got the better of him on this occasion. £10.2m. But a part of it was in share options which came with a time element. The final meeting was in Leeds; the two of us, more of them and solicitors for both parties. Documents duly signed, champagne opened and a toast to our (and their of course, they had a good deal) future; I left feeling that a glorious new chapter in our lives was just beginning. How wrong could I have been?! The old adage "Money is the root of all evil" very soon became a reality.

That weekend Mark didn't want to be in Leeds. The press had got hold of the story and we wanted to keep the children out of any publicity, particularly Rachel. We travelled down to London, taking one of Sam's friends with us, and spent the weekend once again in our favourite hotel, The Grosvenor House on Park Lane. Under the terms of the sale, Mark was required to leave the company immediately but be available for consultation for a period of three months. I still retained my position as H.R. Director and we continued to live more or less as we had done until one Saturday morning in June. For some reason, we must have been on an estate agent's mailing list and upon opening what appeared to be a property update Mark announced that we were to view a property in an exclusive area of Leeds.

Even before we had completed our look around, Mark had decided that he must have the property. We agreed a second viewing with Sam three days later and the deal was sealed.

Mark being Mark he wanted everything perfect before moving in and employed the help of a very well-known interior designer. We were awash with "story boards" and I felt terribly excited and fortunate to have come so far from such humble beginnings.

With all our newfound wealth, D decided to push the boat out (not his of course) for our silver wedding anniversary. We were to host two separate celebrations, one in England and a second in Spain. The venue for celebration number one was Woodhall in Linton. An ideal setting, particularly in the summer months. The hotel was completely taken over for our event. All family, friends in Britain, family in Switzerland and close friends from Europe were to be accommodated over the weekend. No expense was spared. The welcome reception was held on the lawns at the front of the hotel, the weather was perfect, the meal was exquisite, there as a pyramid of champagne for the toast and the entertainment was supplied by none other than Les Dennis which surprised everyone and was thoroughly enjoyed by all. The evening was rounded off by a magnificent firework display and just when I thought that was the finale—Mark pointed down the long driveway. A car was approaching but it was hard to see, in the darkness, which it was. It was my anniversary gift, a brand-new BMW!

Shortly afterwards we set off for Spain but this time it was to our new luxury apartment on the marina within sight of our new and bigger boat! The interior designer had been over with Mark to arrange everything in what seemed a very short space of time. It was gorgeous! Just like a five-star hotel or even better. The terrace went the whole way round the apartment so that all the bedrooms had a balcony and off the living space, there was even room to throw a dinner party which we frequently did. The whole terrace was filled with the scent of the jasmine which was always so beautiful to wake up to in the morning with my coffee.

The following week, we had our second celebration at our favourite hotel in S'Agaro, Spain. Our Spanish and Dutch friends plus half a dozen friends from Britain made up the group. This was absolutely magical.

The dining arrangements were spectacular. Tables had been placed under canvas by the outdoor pool and there were beautiful flower arrangements strategically placed. We were served champagne and cocktails on the lawn before dinner. Everyone had made a special effort as we had specifically stated "evening dress". Dinner jackets and bow ties for the men, although one of our Scottish guests wore a kilt.

The ladies, including myself, had elected to wear long. It was a truly glamour's sight. I really cannot remember the menu now and have lost the invitations along with much of my memorabilia although I still have photographs. After the meal, the hotel had organised an authentic flamenco show which was wonderful—most unlike the ones put on for tourists on package holidays which we had experienced some years ago. The evening was rounded off by dancing on the patio and the younger members of our party heading off to the beach to enjoy midnight skinny-dipping! We spent the rest of the summer in Spain whilst our new home was having a makeover.

We both continued to work for the new owners but several weeks after the sale, Mark was given "garden leave" and his employment terminated. It had been expected of course. However, I still retained my position as HR director. I had always loved my job and cared about the people in our company. I was concerned that their positions would be safe and strove to maintain the "Status Quo". But my contentment was to be short lived.

In early September, Robert came up from the new head office ostensibly for an HR meeting with me regarding the future of personnel. Having spent several weeks detailing the strengths and weaknesses of every member of staff for their future career paths and training, which I duly handed over to him, he quite bluntly told me that my services were no longer required and that I was superfluous to requirements and could I collect my things together and leave immediately! I was devastated! With tears welling up in my eyes, my PA and I hurriedly packed my personal belongings and one or two work related files of my own and I was escorted from the building by the security guard. It was an incredibly sad day as I left the building and company which we had nurtured for almost 20 years!

We had previously planned, before the sale of the company, that we would hold a 20th birthday for the company in September and decided that for the sake and loyalty of the staff, we would go ahead with it. It was held in a local hotel and the theme this time was nautical given that by now Mark's nickname was now "Captain Birdseye". It was a wonderful event and almost 100 per cent of the staff was there. I was happy and sad at the same time, happy to be with them all and see everyone having a great time but sad to know that this would be the last event of its kind as far as we were concerned.

Not too long afterwards, our new home was ready to move into. It was perfect, down to the very last detail. Our interior designer even had a video made which at the time she wanted to use for a TV show. That first weekend our dear friends from Holland came over to "christen" our new home. (Unfortunately, they too are no longer together.) The only person who wasn't happy was Rachel. She had never wanted to leave the home where she had been born and had spent the first 14 years of her life. In retrospect, she was probably right. The house had not brought happiness to at least two of the previous owners and it certainly didn't bring us happiness in the forthcoming years.

After splashing out on our own silver wedding celebrations we decided to give Sam an extra special 18th birthday party. A different venue was required so it was to be Oulton Hall. Once again no expense was spared. The theme was a beach party. Our interior designer and the audio/visual company put their heads together and the set was magical.

The guests all wore beachwear, so many bikini-clad young women! There were cocktails with appropriate names, huge quantities of food, limbo dancing and music till the early hours. The crowning glory was a live guest appearance of the "Honeys". It was yet another of our successful extravaganzas. Unfortunately, the press got hold of it and the headline was something to the effect "What do you give an 18-year-old who has everything? —a party with the Honeys of course!"

With our new home and unexpected wealth, we decided to share some of it with my family in the way of new homes too. My parents lived in a flat with no lift and by now my stepfather was not particularly mobile so we purchased a beautiful, fair sized bungalow for them in a much "better" area. For two of my younger sisters, we invested in a three-bed semi (she was single) and a "family" house for the sister who had three children. I was more than happy to do something for them as my life lacked nothing, or so I thought.

Chapter 17
We Are Millionaires – 2

After what had been an incredibly stressful, if not particularly an enjoyable year, we decided to treat ourselves to a winter in midday January 1999. The Ocean Club in the Bahamas was our destination and the memories of that visit were vividly awakened when watching Daniel Craig in the re-make of Casino Royale. It had been a family holiday but we were accompanied by Sam's then girlfriend and a school friend of Rachel's. Although I enjoyed the luxury of the hotel, but not the long flight there, it was fraught with difficulties. Sam's girlfriend proved to be antisocial and Rachel and her friend would sneak out at night to the nearby Atlantis Hotel for the nightlife and under-age drinking. The only memorable part of the holiday for her except for meeting Cindy Crawford on the beach one day!

Strangely enough, I had always felt slightly guilty about having so much when so many people had far less. We gave large amounts to charity as well as sponsoring various events and giving time, me particularly. I have been a local NSPCC committee member for over 12 years. We had also organised large groups of females to compete in the Race for Life which was a charity to support breast cancer and always followed it by a barbecue-garden party for participants and families.

That year, we were approached by an acquaintance regarding The African Children's Choir. They are a group of African children who tour the world giving concerts in order to raise money, and also awareness, for the education of other African children who are less fortunate. To cut down on expenses, whenever they visit a new venue, they are accommodated in the homes of local people. We played host to three delightful little girls and the following year four equally delightful small boys. They had never been to a supermarket, or done lots of other things for that matter, so Rachel and I initiated them in Tesco. We had trolley races and filled the baskets with a whole manner of foodstuffs they had not seen or eaten before. It was a very gratifying experience. The third year we played host to three boys and one of the young men who travelled with them. Needless to say, when I left the marital home, all this stopped.

One way of Mark hoping to achieve his OBE (yes he really believed he could!) apart from being a successful businessman, and grooming MP's, was pouring money into various charities. His "pet one" was the "Variety Club". A very worthy organisation of which Sarah Ferguson was an active participant.

Our first meeting was totally different to what I had expected. She wasn't the shallow individual portrayed by the media but a genuinely caring, intelligent woman with a great sense of humour. We met on two other occasions and she was kind enough to remember us at Christmas with a beautiful photograph of herself and princesses, Beatrice and Eugenie. Since my separation and subsequent divorce, we have never met again but I have followed her life in the media and then, as now, have always and will always wish her well.

Going to London was always a treat and a pleasure but also an indulgence. First class on the train—breakfast or lunch on the way down and dinner on the return journey. Resident in the Grosvenor House Hotel on the executive floor.

Total freedom to be me and pursue the things that were important to me—theatre, galleries, exhibitions and the occasional shopping mission. This particular trip was a Christmas shopping expedition. The Burlington Arcade was my final destination—Mont Blanc shop in search of a gift for Mark. Hopefully something he wanted and wasn't actually in possession of "difficult" at any time! Gazing out of the window as my selected gift was dutifully wrapped, my eyes focused on a very familiar face. One I had seen only a few days before in Harrogate. It was a difficult face to miss given the accompanying statue. It was none other than Bill Clinton!

Having heard him speak the previous week at a business conference, I felt I really had to speak to him. Rushing out of the shop to the one opposite I was "blocked" by four bodyguards. 'Mr Clinton was doing some Christmas shopping,' I was told. I asked if it would be possible to speak to him and the friendly security said, 'Why not?'

He (Bill Clinton) was so much taller than I realised. I was completely dwarfed and totally smitten. He has an amazing smile and must be one of the most charismatic people I have ever met. That's probably why he attracted, and still does, so much media attention and why his enemies take every opportunity to attack him—from pure jealousy perhaps?

I congratulated him on his speech and he told me he was shopping for things to take home too. The conversation was only about five minutes but I will never, never forget the meeting.

My 40th hadn't been a particularly spectacular event which was partly my fault as I had said that I didn't want a fuss, which of course, I hadn't really meant. My 50th was something very special. We began in London, with half our group, by attending a performance of Oscar Wilde's (my utterly favourite author) "the Importance of being Ernest", followed by a meal but I can't for the life of me remember where, which is most unlike me! The next day, we travelled to Paris and met up with several other friends from Europe. We separated for sightseeing, shopping or whatever everyone felt like doing. In the evening, it was glamour and glitz as we dined at "Manray" and afterwards, had a flutter in the casino which was a short journey outside Paris. But the part that what I enjoyed the most was our Sunday lunch up the Eiffel Tower in the "Jules Verne" restaurant. Superb food and panoramic views of Paris. The weekend was rounded off by our very own carriage on the journey back from London to Leeds with a three-course meal served on board. Magic!

Over the previous two years, I had given up my consultancy work and returned to college. By the summer of 2001, I had managed to obtain two further GCSE and four A-levels and had decided that I would try to fulfil my lifetime ambition of going to university to study English Literature. I duly applied to Oxford University, Harris Manchester College in September of that year. Imagine my delight when I was invited in early November to take an entrance exam. I was absolutely thrilled but very nervous too. We were shown round the college and given lunch in the wonderful dining room and I was confident enough to chat with some of the other candidates. The exam wasn't as difficult as I had expected and I felt that I had done both myself and my lecturers back in Yorkshire justice. Less than two weeks later, I received a letter stating that I had been selected for an interview and I was to spend three days living in the college. I was over the moon. It was an opportunity to pursue something that had been on my mind for many years.

I had decided that the only way, after more than forty years, of reliving the mystery of my father's death was to try to find out the facts for myself. I consulted the family solicitor who obtained a copy of the coroner's report and witness statements. I also asked him to ascertain if anyone involved was still alive and requested that my father's brother be located if indeed he was still alive. I was furnished with the information that my father had taken potassium cyanide in his laboratory at work although he had been found alive and an ambulance was called. Unfortunately he was pronounced dead in the ambulance on Attercliffe Road before reaching the hospital. Apparently his internal injuries were massive. My uncle identified his body.

I was given the address of my uncle who was alive and living in Wantage in Oxfordshire. I wrote to him and told him that I would be in Oxford in early December as I had an interview at Oxford University at Harris Manchester College. And so it was that during the afternoon of one of my three days in Oxford that I took a bus to Wantage and after more than 40 years, met my uncle again. I recognised him, just. He was forty years older and so was I. He made a cup of tea for us both and we chatted about his sons and my family. He then said, 'What is it that you would like to know?'

I told him that I finally wanted the truth, if it had been a suicide, then why? He explained that two weeks before his death, my father and he had had a telephone conversation in which my father had told him he was very worried about work. He had been asked to do something which he believed to be unethical or certainly very dubious. They arranged to speak some time later after my uncle told him 'not to worry' but to think about things, *They never spoke again!*

On the 22nd of December I received a letter from Oxford to say that I had not been successful on this occasion. I was gutted, What a Christmas present! In the New Year, I continued my studies with renewed vigour, determined not to be defeated but to try again later in the year.

By the summer of 2002, it was apparent, to me at least, that our marriage had completely broken down despite our attempts at counselling. We had grown further and further apart, both in interests and activities and our sex life had been almost non-existing for over three years. In part, I believe that was due to me. My studies had gone well and in a remarkably short time, less than two years, I had arranged to obtain two GCSEs and four A levels and had applied to embark on a degree course at university. On the other hand, Mark had channelled his energies into hosting "boys" trips on his new boat to various locations in the Mediterranean whilst at the same time buying several properties in Whitby with a view to a seaside letting business and also becoming owner of a clothing company which was to be his financial downfall some years later.

It was on one of my frequent visits to my sister in Switzerland in November of that year that I finally made my decision to ask for a divorce.

Things were particularly strained at home, Sam having left and settled in a cottage a couple of miles away. Rachel by this time had progressed to hard drugs and my attempt to have her made a ward of court or get professional help had fallen on deaf ears with Mark.

I had applied to university for the following year and was invited to take an exam for Oxford again. I was invited for an interview again but unfortunately just before Christmas I received a letter saying I had been unsuccessful. I was absolutely devastated as I had felt that I had a good chance (as I did my lecturers). However, I was accepted by four other universities the following January.

I think Christmas Eve was actually the turning point of what could have been, if there ever is one, an amicable divorce. It was after midnight and I was still wrapping presents and making last minute preparation for the following day when Rachel arrived home. She was like someone possessed. She flew at me, hammering me with her fists and hurling abuse at me her language was appalling. As I staggered to my feet to avoid her blows, she ran to the kitchen and returned with a knife screaming she would kill me.

I made for the front door and towards the gates. Mark, as ineffectual as ever, tried to talk her around but she was having none of it. (It wasn't until much later that I found out what had precipitated this violent and abusive behaviour.) Apparently, for the sum of £150, she had been asked to obtain some "coke" for a third party. Not being content with the money, she had helped herself to some of it. It is one at the most frightening and saddening experience to see one's child reduced to that state. But what is even worse is having no support from one's husband—in fact the complete opposite!

Late as it was I called my brother-in-law and he immediately told me to call the police. It was not only my person she was attacking; she had hurled a brick at my parked car.

The police arrived and tried to calm the situation. It was decided that we shouldn't spend the night under the same roof. Mark wanted me to check into a hotel but I was adamant that after everything that I had endured, I was staying put. Rachel called her boyfriend and went to stay there.

The following morning, Christmas Day, I packed an overnight bag and drove to my sister's to spend the day in peace. As I was leaving, true to form, selfish and self-centred to the last. Mark said, 'Who is going to cook Christmas lunch?'

And so it was that I spent a wonderfully peaceful and happy Christmas day with my sister and her family in Rotherham. I returned the following day to pick up some food and wine and accepted solace with one of my college teachers (female) and the evening in the casino.

Upon returning home, I continued to sleep in one of the guest rooms, keeping it locked during the night, although by this time, Rachel had removed herself to her boyfriend's house.

In early January 2003, Mum and Bob (my new stepfather) had taken advantage of a long stay Saga holiday to Almeria in Spain and I had booked an overland trip to visit them for a week. It would be a long journey but I wasn't prepared to fly, particularly alone. However, before I was due to leave for Spain, something much unexpected happened.

Chapter 18
A Passionate Affair

On our, well my really, frequent visits to the casino, I was in the habit of talking to one of the waiters. It was partly to practice my French, as he was Algerian and let's face it, partly because I found him attractive. On this particular evening, we exchanged mobile numbers with a view to meeting for a coffee and some French conversation. The following day, to my surprise, he called and asked if we could meet that evening at 7:30, as it was his night off. I agreed immediately but having done so, I began to realise that I could have a problem getting out of the house. Mark and I had agreed to separate and divorce but things weren't easy. At 6 o'clock, I went upstairs, had a bath dressed with extra care and slipped back downstairs. I grabbed my French file and car keys. As I opened the front door, Mark growled, 'Where are you going?'

'I'm meeting some other students for a French conversation class!' I shouted, as I made a hasty exit.

My heart was beating fast and I felt dizzy with excitement and a certain amount of trepidation as I drove into the city centre. Ish wasn't there when I first drove past the elected meeting place. Drat! However, on my second circuit of the block, I saw his solitary figure. *Too gorgeous*, I thought, never having seen him without his waiter's garb. We parked the car and Ish suggested a small Spanish bistro, five minutes' walk away. Apparently, one of his friends was a waiter there. We sat at the bar and he ordered our drinks. He lit a cigarette and offered me one. 'No, thank you, I gave up years ago,' I said. We were shown to a quiet table and given a menu. We ordered a light meal as I was a confirmed member of "Slimming World" at the time. After we had eaten, he took both my hands across the table. I looked into his face and he said, 'It's to stop me smoking.'

I drove him home at eleven, parked nearby his flat and turned off the engine. He turned towards me and I turned to face him. He took me in his arms and began to kiss me. Gently at first and then it became more passionate. It was a wonderful feeling. I hadn't been kissed for so long and I was crying out for physical affection. I knew we both wanted to take it further but I refused his request to go home with him given my current situation.

Whilst Mark and I had agreed to divorce, it was on the grounds that we had grown apart not because there was anyone else involved. During this time, Sam had been helping me to find a new home to move to as I was still sleeping in one of the guest rooms.

Ish and I agreed to meet again the following evening but this time, I knew exactly what was going to happen. The next afternoon, for the first time in my life, I found myself in Tesco buying condoms. I had no idea what to get so I just picked up two packets, blue being my favourite colour. At the checkout, for some reason, I turned bright red as the cashier put through my purchases. It could have been guilt but I rather think it was a mixture of being found out and the prospect of the evening.

We met close to Ish's flat but instead of going for a drink or a meal, we went straight there. He had, being a waiter, remembered what I always drank—sparkling water, lemon, and no ice. We chatted for a while on the sofa and when the necking became too much for both of us, he suggested we go to the bedroom. It was the first time I had had sex for a long time and it was truly beautiful. He was kind, gentle and a complete turn-on. We had sex three times during the course of the evening. I didn't have to admit to buying condoms. He was obviously more prepared than me.

After two weeks of our "secret meetings" I moved in with him. I was still going home to collect clothes etc. and working part-time. It was an incredibly happy time for me. I had never felt so much love, or so I thought, for a single person except my children. We shared the cooking although I did the washing and ironing. Ish's flat was nothing like the palatial home I had turned my back on. It was a council flat in a high-rise block and under normal circumstances somewhere I would never dream of going anywhere near but these weren't normal circumstances! We spent several weekends in a holiday cottage in Whitby even taking my niece and nephews with us two weekends. Ish met my mother and everyone who met him was quite taken with him. We seemed to have so much in common despite the huge age difference; I was actually virtually old enough to be his mother! He helped with my French homework and sometimes we would speak in French so that I could practice. I spoke to his best friend in Paris on the phone and we made various plans for the future including spending a week on the boat later in the year which was to have been part of my divorce settlement. I even bought him a car to make travelling to work easier, especially when he was working night shifts which was quite often.

However, my newfound happiness was interrupted by my visit to see Mum and Bob in Almeria. I travelled by train from Leeds to London and then on to Paris where I took the overnight sleeper into Spain. It was an incredible journey as I was travelling first class, of course! The changes of scenery were varied and interesting and slightly different from the train journey across Europe to Switzerland which I had done several times. I changed trains in Madrid at Atocha Station, the scene of the dreadful bombing which rocked the country, little thinking that one day I would be living in that very city. Upon arrival in Almeria, it was a bus ride to Rocquetas where Mum and Bob were staying. During the journey, a young Moroccan struck up a conversation with me which passed the time and he was able to help me find a taxi when we arrived in the town centre. It was late evening when I finally arrived at the hotel and eventually found Mum and Bob in the bar after depositing my luggage in the room. I spent an idyllic relaxing week there and even had a couple of dinner dates, one with the Moroccan whose name turned out to be Rashid. I left feeling very happy and relaxed.

However, upon my return to England not everything was rosy. Mark put a private detective on to me and the abusive phone calls on both sides began to tell on my mental state. I began to have dizzy spells and virtual blackouts, loss of memory and several physical stress symptoms. On two occasions, Ish took me to the A and E department but they said they could find nothing wrong with me. At the time, I was being prescribed Seroxin, which I found out much later can sometimes have dire side effects. My neurosis escalated and some days I just couldn't get out of bed or leave the flat. Things are very hazy about that time but I do know that Ish had to call Sam numerous times as he was so worried about me. I remember being "rescued" from a Chinese restaurant as I felt I was being followed by a female spy who had also been in the same coffee bar that day. The white van with the listening equipment was always in the vicinity. If I did go out, I was convinced that the white van was following me trying to keep surveillance on Ish who by then I believed was a spy or something to do with the Iraqi war. I also became utterly convinced that he and his compatriots, whoever they may be, were trying to steal my identity for terrorist purposes. I found clothes missing and then I was convinced that he had stolen my passport too. Things got so bad that one day when he brought me a meal in bed and spread a striped blanket under it I thought he was going to take a photograph to use in a kidnap plot!

I remember waking up feeling that my head wasn't on my body. I had a floating sensation and it was difficult to focus. Ish was still in bed. I looked out of the window and saw the familiar white van which I thought was "stalking" us—MI5 or terrorists having some connection with Ish. The mysterious briefcases (which eventually turned out to be sets of cutlery) in the spare bedroom I was convinced were bombs waiting to be detonated in some strategic location in Britain. My head was pounding as I opened the front door and, still in my pyjamas, started walking towards the main road and "safety". The car of one of Rachel's friend's parents drew up beside me rolling down the windows and saying, 'Are you alright? Can I give you a lift?' I declined the offer. By now I was suspicious and afraid of everyone. Suddenly I realised that Ish was following me. I increased my speed, seeing him too as the enemy. As he approached to within several yards of me, I remember screaming, 'Please, don't kill me, Ish. Please don't kill me.' He tried to reason with me but by now I was attracting a lot of attention from vehicles and passers-by. I ran across the road to a nearby shop where I knew an ex-colleague now worked. She gave me a cup of coffee and endeavoured to calm me down asking if there was anyone she could call. I think she must have called Sam but I can't honestly remember. I believe that Ish then came to collect me and took me home to wait for Sam.

Chapter 19
Sectioned

On the afternoon of 5th April, 2003, Sam and I arrived at a private clinic in Harrogate for my appointment. After a short interview and some discussion between the doctor and Sam, it was agreed that I should be sectioned for 28 days (the minimum I believe).

Ish was interviewed by the consultant too and whether it was because he was a Muslim like himself, he denied that we were an item, that we were living together and stated that he had given me a bed as I had nowhere to go. He failed to include the fact that it was HIS bed and that we had sex and made love almost every day. For it certainly was love on my part, or had I been fooling myself and it was total infatuation due to the fact that he was young—well youngish— handsome, intelligent and I was old enough to be his mother. At this point, one of my Rolex watches and some other expensive jewellery were handed over to Sam as it was inappropriate for such valuable items to be kept at the clinic. Ish and Sam left me in what was to be my "home" for the next nine weeks and to possibly one of the most harrowing experiences of my entire life.

I was shown to my accommodation—a single room with an on-suite bathroom. The surroundings were pleasant enough, definitely four-star, paid by BUPA of course. I sat on the edge of my bed, my vision still blurred; everything jumbled; nothing making sense—fear, sadness, anger. How had I come to be in such a situation? It was probably obvious to anyone who knew both me and my circumstances. The hounding and persecution and the abusive phone calls I had received since meeting Ish during the past few weeks from Mark had finally taken its toll.

The first few weeks were quite hazy. I was totally "out of it". With all the medication, I remember having some meals in my room before I was allowed to join the other patients in the dining room, Sam visited but I don't recall his early visits. Mark actually had the gall to send flowers during the first week. One of the side effects of my various medications was "walking legs". My legs just wouldn't stop jumping and twitching; the pain was terrible, and I had to keep walking about for ages to gain any relief.

However, a constant visitor was Freddie, a so-called "friend" of Sam's. For some strange reason, I had called him sometime after being admitted. It was probably "the" biggest mistake of my life as I was to find out and to this day wherever I think of him, although I try not to, my blood boils and I have nothing but sheer hatred towards him for what he did to me and on really bad days, wish him nothing but harm. But more of that later.

My sister, brother-in-law and nephew were over from Switzerland as they had planned to spend a week with Ish and I. I was so sorry not to be there to welcome them but Ish took charge of that and the shopping. They visited every day until

131

they left for London on their way back home. I can only remember my mother coming once and one of my sisters. Mental problems seem to be extremely difficult for the majority of people to deal with. Consequently, my best friend of over 25 years and her husband virtually disowned me which saddened me no end. I now realise that it must have been a very shallow friendship.

I believe I did have short periods of lucidity but they were few and far between in those first few weeks. I gleaned some details from my mother and doctors later. Apparently, I had been extremely ill. I still had hallucinations and delusions and lived in a fantasy world. Mentally, I regressed years and was known to have picnics with soft toys on my bedroom floor. I danced in the corridor to the same music over and over again and wrote practically daily which I realised was totally rubbish months later.

During this time, I was under the legal protection of the courts as I was deemed unfit to deal with my own affairs—namely my divorce. Freddie visited every day and dealt with my laundry and any items of shopping I may have needed—mostly cigarettes as I had started smoking again after 18 years. He also took away my remaining Rolex watch which he said was to go in his mother's safe for some reason.

Sam came almost daily too. Ish never came back to the clinic. Apparently, he had been told it was bad for me and detrimental to my recovery, a decision which I have always believed had just the opposite effect. I went on hunger strike for a few days in the hope that Ish would be allowed to visit but to no avail.

The weeks passed and on the day that my "section" was ended, I intended to leave and called Sam to collect me. My consultant had other plans. When he heard that I was trying to discharge myself, I was physically prevented from doing so—in fact I was manhandled to my bed and forcibly injected, with what I don't know, before passing out. The following day, I was informed that I still wasn't fit to join the outside world. Retrospectively, I feel there were far more "crazier" people, at liberty, than me. Three more weeks passed and I was told that I could leave but would be an outpatient.

I was so relieved and never wanted to see the inside of that place again.

I went home which had now been vacated by Ish but my mood was buoyant although I missed him terribly. I seemed to be on a complete high. I had decided that I was going to build a school, a church and a hospital in Uganda. What planet was I on???

I duly rang round family, friends (yes I still had some then) and acquaintances (and those too at the time) soliciting volunteers for a trip to Uganda in the coming October. At the same time, informing them I was anticipating acquiring a plane from British Airways and funds from other sources for the project.

When I look back, I wonder if those people actually believed me or were they still placating my "illness". Several days later, at one of my outpatient appointments, I was confronted by my consultant regarding my planned project. Didn't I feel this was a totally unreasonable expectation? he asked: To which I replied, 'No, not really.'

Having received this response, he proceeded to tell myself and Sam that I was certainly still 'ill' and would have to be readmitted! And so my "mission" was cancelled although I'm sure Uganda has managed quite well without my help. After another 10 days as a resident, my stay came to an abrupt end. The Bupa money had run out! I was helped to pack and transferred, with hardly any notice at all, to a psychiatric unit in Leeds. It was a far cry from the luxury of the clinic in Harrogate but the treatment I received was infinitely better.

At first, I just used to lay on my bed, I wasn't allowed out of the unit. My sister visited once and Rachel actually visited too. Sam and Jane came more often or Sam on his own. However, my constant visitor was the notorious FRA (I have since renamed him Fucking Rip-off Animal). He proceeded to tell me that my family in Rotherham didn't really want me and where would I be without him. Well, now that I am of a supposedly sound mind, I know I would have been a damn sight better off, both financially and personally!

In an environment with others in a similar situation, or in fact some worse, it is easy to make superficial friendships and towards the end of my incarceration I actually had some happy days. Sneaking off to Asda down the road and pooling our money for alcohol, making a fire in the woods and sitting drinking, and even on one occasion smoking pot, and talking until bed-time were special and helped to relieve the monotony. It was also during that time that I decided to become a Muslim like Ish. I stopped eating pork and insisted on covering my head and neck with various coloured scarves, frequenting the continental shops whenever possible and generally making a complete idiot of myself as I now realise. My family was very understanding and played along with my whims, due to the imbalance of my mind, even on occasions taking me to obtain my bizarre purchases. It was the middle of July when I was finally allowed back into the community. It was also during my time at Seacroft that I struck up a friendship with Alan, an Iraqui refugee from Ish's block of flats. Perhaps relationship is not the right word. When I was allowed out, I would take a taxi to his flat for the sole purpose of having sex. Obviously I was still not well!

Chapter 20
Depths of Despair

Back to a house that held all the memories of Ish. I ached all the time and felt totally bewildered and lost.

Why had it happened to me? Would I ever feel like a real human being again? I had no confidence or self-esteem. I was at rock bottom. The house felt too big and far too empty as did my life. How would I begin to exist again and function as I had done previously before all this? The answer is that I didn't.

I had daily visits from Freddie and we would usually go out in his disgusting white van or my car. Sam and his friend sometimes called in the evenings only to find me listening to Algerian music and making up dance routines. Once or twice, we even had trips to the coast but they were supposed to be kept secret from his wife, as were many other things! Such as his numerous "flings" and our trip to Paris with one of his "amours". At least I got to go to the "Moulin Rouge" and drink champagne. I always had to eat out as I was still beyond shopping or cooking. I would call friends (the ones I still had) to arrange to have dinner instead of being alone at home. There were occasional overnight stays in Rotherham with family to break the sheer boredom and monotony of my life. And I was supposed to be well!

I was lonely and miserable so one evening, a friend and I decided to attend a local singles evening where I met Ralph. Another strange relationship as we only met when he wanted sex and there was still Alan, who would come round sometimes to spend the night even though for me the sex was shit—just something to pass the time. I had really sunk to great depths by then.

I did see Ish once but only in the presence of Freddie and it was so painful that I couldn't think of anything else for weeks. Sometimes Sam and his friend would call round to check on me or I would spend a Sunday afternoon at Sam 's watching a film or occasionally, we would go to the cinema or for a meal but even so I just wasn't functioning as I had done before my breakdown. Couldn't the doctors see that?

The small club I had purchased for Sam had died a death, it turned out not to be such a viable proposition after all and he was searching for something else in which to invest and hopefully make a success of. He found a club in nearby Wakefield but the problem was a matter of funding. And so it was decided that I would sell my home and move to a smaller property out in the country, in the next village to Freddie and his family and purchase the club for Sam out of the profit from the sale of my home. I agreed willingly as I thought it would solve both Sam's and my problems. His need for investment and my need to be closer to Freddie. But that was not the case unfortunately. It certainly worked out for Sam but not for me! The new home for me was less than half the size of my previous home. It was a small cottage in a village with one shop and two pubs. It was too small for all my lovely furniture; it had no shower, the plumbing was shocking with the toilet often overflowing onto the bathroom floor, shit, paper and all. The bedroom was too small for a bed, it was actually a mattress on a raised plinth and the staircase was so steep that I needed to hold on to the rope handrail whenever I went upstairs.

I can honestly say, hand on heart, what was left of it, that the cottage however quaint it may sound, was by far the worst place I have ever lived in, up to and since then… And I did all this for the sake of my son. Having said that, I would do it all over again without a second thought for the most important person in my life—Sam.

I had neither the will nor the inclination to shop and therefore, the only commodity that was readily available was wine—of course. No coffee in the morning as there was never any milk. I did manage, however, to secure necessities such as loo rolls. I would wake early, usually hung over, and had to have the requisite two Anadins and water before I could function at all. Then a bath in which I could barely fit. I think the previous owners must have been pygmies! I then had to wait the arrival of the infamous, but who I believed at that time to be my saviour, Freddie.

The day consisted of travelling around in his disgusting white van, of which I must say he was inordinately proud, but it was more like a rusty mobile dustbin. We usually called at Mc Donald's which was my brunch and the highlight of most days. This would be followed by visits to various "business" associates. The word business is in parenthesis as they were a motley crew and the business was not always legitimate, I believe. Fake handbags, watches and whatever could be traded was traded and there was I thinking I couldn't sink any lower, that I was already at the bottom of the cess pit! Oh, how the other half live!

I frequently asked if I could have the return of my Rolex watch but there was always some excuse, he also forced me to hand over my diamond eternity ring which he wanted for his partner and "bought" my ruby ring from me at a ridiculous price.

Sam's new club premises had to undergo a certain amount of renovation but "opening night" finally arrived. It was a great success and eventually led to a small empire for Sam. I was extremely proud of him, and still am for that matter.

In March of that year, I was lifted out of the situation for a week when I paid for two friends to accompany me to Tenerife. The hotel was excellent, the weather not so and the two friends definitely did not gel! Not the best scenario for a great holiday! We were told that the Salsa club was the place to go and where the talent was. Jaine and I did secure males of a sort and I ended up inviting mine back to the hotel. It was a strange relationship as he spoke no English and my Spanish at that pretty basic. However, any port in a storm. I did in fact return to the island twice more to continue the strange union. My last visit was as a "smuggler" of sorts. Freddie sent someone to accompany me and we were to return with several thousand cigarettes to sell in England. Unfortunately, the customs in Manchester had cottoned on and they were all confiscated. As they weren't in my luggage, I was exonerated.

Over the next few months, I managed to sink even lower. I picked up my association with Adom and had a very brief relationship with Winston whom I met in one of Leeds' town centre pubs. That all ended when after a lunchtime drinking session, I decided to drive to another pub. I hit the kerb,

Winston jumped out and I proceeded on to the motorway only to be stopped, breathalysed and kept in a police cell for several hours before being driven home at 2:30 in the morning. I was fined 250 pounds and lost my license for 15 months which was pretty fair under the circumstances.

During these months, I tried to rekindle old friendships. One couple who had been missionaries in Africa prior to our meeting completely cut me off. Some Christians! And I later found out that Horacen the husband was having two affairs at the same time as still being with his wife. Double standards I feel! The weeks wore on and then it was decided yet again, that I would be better off living even closer to Freddie and his family. I was to sell the cottage and buy a bungalow which had "accommodation" for me in the garden. When I actually saw it, I was terror-struck! It was a brick building—one room—no bathroom. There was no room for the little furniture I had been left with and yet again it was miles from civilisation as I knew it. What could I do? Before I had to sign the papers, I voiced my misgivings but Freddie burst into floods of tears saying, 'How can you do this to my wife and the children?' That was it. With no other help to call on, the dastardly deed was done. They had the bungalow modernised, furnished and moved in before Christmas leaving me "high and dry" alone in the cottage again. So every time I think my life can't get any worse, I know from past experience, that it can, and it does! Christmas and New Year came and went like any other day. 2005… What would it bring for me?

Chapter 21
Switzerland, 2005

After nine months of enduring this type of isolated, humiliating and positively degenerate lifestyle, apart from being robbed blind and treated like a complete imbecile, I was thrown a "life-line", a float in the murky waters of my existence. I felt like a triumphant survivor of the "Titanic"!

On a late January visit to my sister's in Switzerland as my brief but happy escape was coming to an abrupt end, I decided, well I didn't really choose for myself, it all came pouring out, to offload the misery and grief of the past 12 months. No sooner had these startling revelations computed in the brains of my sister and her husband, they were on the telephone to various family members in England, and so my year-long stay in the land of gnomes, holey cheese and Milka chocolate began. It was a blissful time for me but I dare say, with hindsight, a difficult and stressful time for the Swiss family "B". I can honestly say, hand on heart, that my brother-in-law Pierre was, and is, the most genuine, kind-hearted, sympathetic, level-headed, positive, super-intelligent man I have ever known. There are not enough superlatives to describe him. Obviously, some of the many reasons my sister married him.

For me, it was a tremendous learning process, from taking care of myself to re-finding my cooking skills, though several dishes frequently missed the mark, rendering once palatable ingredients inedible, to rediscovering the washing machine and iron, not least of all, to re-establishing communication with other intelligent members of the human race.

The first three months flew by in a haze of helping with any sister's beautiful twins and my amazing bi-lingual nephew, grocery shopping, long walks and trying to perfect my already good French. I had to return to England on two occasions for meetings with my solicitors as I had now managed to sell and clear the cottage. However, when I did return to pack up, I found my sapphire ring, my wedding ring, my jade and jet jewellery and all my other jewellery that was worth anything missing along with items of expensive clothing and some personal possessions. The only other person who had a key to the cottage apart from myself was, you've guessed, Freddie! One day soon, I will try to do something about it as there were also forged cheques and bills for things I most certainly never had. Luckily I still have the receipt for my Rolex watch, bank statements and copy cheques!

In March, my ever-perceptive brother-in-law suggested that I take an extended French course at Bien University which once again in my life brought about a change which was to colour, for use of a pun, the rest of my life. I enjoyed the course immensely and not only did it improve my French so that I was able to hold four hours conversations in total French (of which I am still extremely proud) but it also introduced me to Rosemary who was a true friend during my time in Switzerland and led to meeting Paul, who was hopefully to become my life-long partner. It was one Tuesday evening. Whilst travelling by train to one of my classes I found myself staring into the face of a young (compared to me) black man. (A "black-as-your-hat face" as my grandmother used to say. Were all hats black in her time?) and heard the words, 'I'm Paul. What's your name?'

To which I replied, 'Christine.'

'And are you a Christian?' was his next question.

During the following conversation, I was informed that he was attending a two-week rally at a local church. He asked me to meet him for a drink after my class but I declined several times, not knowing how my sister would react and partly because I'd never had contact with anyone quite so black! However, eventually I agreed to call my sister and tell her that I would take a later train.

It was the quietest "first date" I had ever had and I was quite relieved when 40 minutes later, it was time to catch the train back to Swiss suburbia and safety.

However, it didn't end there. Next morning, while I was in the village with the twins on our daily excursion, I received a text message offering the hand of friendship and extolling the virtues of Jesus. I'm not sure, to this day, why I agreed, but after clearing things with my sister, I found myself arranging to meet at 7:30 pm that evening in the next village.

He was there to meet the train, which of course, in Switzerland, arrives precisely when it was scheduled to. He said that he had bought food and drinks so we were to walk to his "house". House is in parenthesis as it did not exactly denote his possession or indeed conform to the description of house. It was in fact a large building which contained a number of rooms on two floors which were inhabited by other individuals mostly from the African continent.

The room was no bigger than a hotel bathroom containing, amazingly, a set of bunk beds, a large fridge, TV, DVD player, a sink and a white plastic chair. Well, there was certainly no space for anything else!

He was politeness itself having purchased and previously chilled a bottle of rosé wine and a selection of snacks. The choice was the white plastic chair or the bottom bunk. I chose the chair. The window was permanently covered by a dingy, striped curtain and there was minimal light reminding me of the numerous grubby bedsits of the 50s and 60s in miniature obviously!

After on hour of fact-finding, listening to music and at least one bottle of wine, he removed the mattress from the bottom bunk where he had been sitting and placed it on the floor and proceeded to lie fully stretched on it with his arms behind his head as though he was on some beach back in Africa. As I stood to take in this bizarre scene, he said, 'Dishabille?' to which I replied, 'Pardon?' For a moment, having lost any connection with the French language altogether. 'Undress,' was how it was repeated in English. Meek as a lamb, I duly undressed and lay down beside him on the mattress.

The room was warm but I was even warmer. Not from the internal temperature but from the touch of another human being on my naked body. It had been so long since I had experienced such male closeness. He suddenly got up and went to what could only be described as his wardrobe. After taking out something, which I couldn't see, he undressed and lay down again. In the warm glow from the light above the white utilitarian sink, I could make out the shape of his beautiful, young black body and I was filled with anticipation. I had never been a great admirer of the white male, for some reason, particularly uncircumcised, but this "vision" was totally contrary. His skin was smooth and soft and his body so well-proportioned with a beautiful circumcised male organ. I had often heard that black men had bigger penises but in this case, I'm sure it was a fallacy as his was, to my mind, the perfect size, neither too big nor too small to perform its many functions.

As he began kissing and caressing my naked, waiting body, I realised that what he had retrieved from the wardrobe was in fact a condom, which he skilfully donned and before I knew it, with my legs splayed, one still on the mattress and the other jacked-up on the sink; he entered my eagerly expectant body. This was the first night of many and the more I got to know him or about him, I realised he was a kind, gentle, generous, sensitive, caring and surprisingly enough a 32-year-old virgin! However, I wasn't exclusive at the time and did have a one-night stand with one of his friends and a cosy weekend with a Serb!

Our relationship continued (even though after several weeks, I revealed my true age) during the course of my stay in Switzerland. I fell in love with him and it was reciprocated to the point of deep adoration and respect. Perhaps it was because he had no other relationship to compare it with.

Who's to know how the human heart works? He had wanted to be ordained but had neither the money nor the education, having been the breadwinner for the family back home since his early teens. He had also made a conscious decision not to bring any children into the world which was a good job really since I had had to be sterilised after Rachel's birth.

On Christmas Eve, it was with mixed feelings that I said goodbye to the picturesque Swiss chalet and its five inhabitants. I was to spend the next four days, before returning to England, with in a hotel in a neighbouring village. It was a perfect Christmas in so many ways. It was picture postcard Switzerland. Snow covering the rooftops, trees and nearby mountains. It also happened to be the first time I had spoken to Sam for almost 10 months!

On Christmas Day, shortly after lunch, I sent Sam a text message wishing him happy birthday and a Merry Christmas. Imagine my surprise and sheer delight when less than two minutes later, my phone rang and it was Sam. I was incredibly happy and we spoke for almost half an hour. I had been banned from speaking to him whilst I was living in Switzerland due to personal and financial issues which he had been blamed for. I never felt like that. He was my son, my flesh and blood whatever he did, had done or was likely to do. My very special Christmas present all those years ago. We agreed that in the New Year when I was back in England, we would meet up to catch up, I couldn't wait and so I said *adieu* to Paul at the station and returned to England.

Chapter 22
Return to England
and Divorce, 2006

My return to England, Yorkshire in fact, was not only tinged with sadness at leaving such a wonderful family, and of course Paul, but was a complete culture shock compared to what I had left behind. Of course, they didn't speak French, but what did they speak? My ears were completely unaccustomed and un-tuned to the accent and dialect which engulfed me.

It was agreed that I was to live in my mother's house as she was on holiday with Bob for a further few weeks. After living in a busy, comforting family for so long, being told that I had to live in a strange house, unfamiliar town totally alone filled me with horror. Added to this, the financial hearing and divorce proceedings were imminent. But every cloud has a silver lining and that month I met and saw Sam for the first time in almost 12 months. The joy was two-fold as he told me over lunch that he was to be a parent later in the year—and me a grandmother. Wow!

My brother-in-law (English one of course) was allowed to attend the hearing with me at the high court in London, in late

January. It was the first time that I had seen Mark in over a year and I felt like a party jelly—wibble, wobble. Although I didn't look like one as I had lost over three stones during my stay in Switzerland due to my sister's encouragement.

It wasn't as traumatic as I had expected but at one point, I had to be offered a glass of water as I was in danger of passing out. Most of what was said, discussed and agreed is still a blur but I do know that the eventual outcome was supposed to be a reasonable income for life, a home to be purchased with money for furniture, etc.

That's what the court decided, but as will be seen later Mark has always been a law unto himself.

I didn't take long to find the perfect property. A flat in a new block called the Limes. They were built on what used to be the old Limes Hotel years ago which I had visited when J was a guest on one of his visits to the Abbey National in Rotherham. How strange life is! I continued to live with my mother and Bob whilst waiting for the flat sale to be completed but it was a particularly difficult time for all concerned. But Bob was prone to constant mood swings. One minute he was all right, the next he was trying to find me other accommodation. My stress incontinence, which had begun shortly after my breakdown, became so bad, coupled with my excessive drinking that there was hardly a night that I didn't wet the bed. I began to spend a lot of time playing bingo—and not often winning—which is where I met and got to know Emma who became a god-send in the months and years to come. Eventually, contracts were signed and the flat became mine, or so I thought. The next few weeks were spent buying furnishings and making a home I thought would be permanent, yet another miscalculation! It was never to be in my name, but what a surprise, another example of Mark's wheeling and dealing and total disregard for the law.

The bed-wetting became extremely difficult to hide until one day when I was out my mother had occasion, probably to snoop, to go into my bedroom. All hell let loose when I arrived home. I had ruined the mattress for which I had to pay next morning. I also found all my belongings packed into every available box and bag and anything else that was available and was transported a few miles to my flat—ready or not.

I spent several weeks unpacking what seemed an endless stream of boxes, bags and containers, receiving curtains and some items of furniture. The best of which was, still is, an Italian glass dining table with wrought iron chairs which Sam purchased for me on Mother's Day a few months earlier.

The flat served its purpose as somewhere to eat, sleep and watch TV but I missed Paul so much. I worried about him and didn't know when we would see each other again. Everything seemed like a chore, cooking, cleaning, eating, shopping and I felt so lonely.

However, a few weeks later, I received a phone from Paul to say that he had moved to Paris.

I arranged to meet him the following weekend and duly booked my train tickets (I wasn't going to fly, was I?) I chose an Etap Hotel which was fairly central and had good transport connections (I know Paris better than I knew/know London due to my many visits there). I travelled laden with what I hoped would be enough food for four days. I have always loved Paris but this visit was quite magical. Up at the crack of dawn every morning. I played the part of the tourist guide. The Eiffel Tower, Tuilerie Gardens, Notre Dame,

Montmartre, Sacre Coeur, a boat trip on the Seine, pavement cafés. We crammed so much into those four days. But the nights were for our "sights". No matter how long we were apart for, being together was like falling in love all over again. It was also the first time we had a shower together (but not the last).

The walk-in showers in the Etap Hotel are ideal for sex in the shower. And so, yet another fond farewell and a return to England. But at least I had something to look forward to Sam and June's wedding.

It was a difficult few day. I experienced so many mixed emotions. Excitement about the trip and a chance to get away from my situation, apprehension about telling my family where I was going and for what reason and dread regarding a 10-hr flight. My sister and brother-in-law were very philosophical about the revelation. 'No contest, a week in Las Vegas or a week in Rotherham?' It was indeed no contest!

It was a small group of us that left Manchester early that June morning. (Sam, J's sister and three friends, June's brother followed later). I was Sam's only relative as Mark refused to go as did Rachel. In fact, I haven't seen her since January 2005 when I began my stay in Switzerland, but who knows, one day she will grow up and come to realise that there were faults on both sides—not just mine. (Not forgetting hers of course!)

We were booked into the well-known Hotel Bellagio (of Oceans' 11 fame). I thoroughly enjoyed my first trip to Vegas. The hotel was truly amazing and I was able to spend time with Sam. The "Strip" has to be seen to be believed, no photographs or other people's descriptions can truly capture the sights, sounds and smells of it. However, as you can imagine in June, it was incredibly hot and most of the party spent the day by the pool or in the spa. As with all hotels in Vegas, the lobby is awash with one-armed bandits and I must admit to becoming quite addicted but never did win my fortune! We ate out most of the time and I think my favourite was the Lebanese restaurant closely followed by the Chinese one.

The wedding was quite, quite different from any other I had attended. But true to form Sam and were late even to that. The ceremony was performed on the "Starship Enterprise", aliens and all! This was followed by a trip to a funfair and a Chinese meal.

It was a short but well needed release from my humdrum existence.

However, the return to England was somewhat marred by the fact that my (Sam went off to the Bahamas) flight was cancelled and I had to wait in another hotel for two days before I was booked on a flight back to Manchester via Seattle with a six-hour stopover.

Over the next few months, Paul and I communicated by telephone but I wasn't as miserable as usual as I had the impending birth of my first grandchild to look forward to. At the beginning of September, Paul called to say that he was now in Spain and that I should join him as soon as possible, as through a friend, he had managed to rent a shared house in a small town in Murcia. My totally beautiful granddaughter was born on the 6th of September and five days later, I left for Murcia.

Chapter 23
Murcia

And so it was that I left for Murcia for what was intended to be an eight-week holiday with Paul. He had rented a room in a house in El Palmar, a town 40 minutes' journey inland from the airport which friends living in the area had told him about. It was sun, sex but definitely no sand! He was waiting at the airport with two friends who lived in a neighbouring town. I was so happy to see him after several months apart; I didn't care about where we were to live. The room was in a second floor flat which we were to share with another African. We had our own bedroom but unfortunately the "bed" was a mattress on the floor with no bedding. We shared the sitting room, bathroom and kitchen with Eddie; we even had our own shelves in the fridge! The first few days we didn't venture outside the flat. Eddie worked all day and we spent our time eating, drinking and having lots of sex. On the mattress, on the floor, on the sofa but the kitchen was out of bounds because of all the cockroaches (who eventually migrated to the bathroom too after several weeks); if you banged the cupboard doors in the kitchen, they would all come falling down on the worktop!

We spent our eight weeks idyllically together. I was the proper little housewife, shopping, cooking, washing, ironing, and all the normal things. But Paul always went to the supermarket with me as a bag carrier. We had a favourite bar in the town where we would go most days for coffee or breakfast and read the newspapers or watch TV. The landlord had disconnected the TV and music system so that we were unable to use it. After several weeks, he was persuaded to let us have the use of them as we were paying the electricity bills anyway. We would sometimes take a bus ride into the city to window shop and even have a pizza on occasions. It was an incredibly happy time regardless of the living conditions. We were together at last and that was all that mattered. And then it was time for me to leave.

We decided that I would return and try to find more suitable accommodation as the landlord had rented his bedroom (and which had the only bed) to another couple refusing to let us change. And so after returning to England and discussions with Sam, it was agreed that I should return to Spain in two weeks and seek suitable living accommodation for which Sam would contribute half.

We were lucky enough to find a beautiful three-bed roomed, refurbished flat in a small village just a few miles away after being turned down by our first choice because Paul was black! The owner made no bones about it—just said, 'I don't want him,' in Spanish of course. This was just the first of many instances where we encountered racial prejudice in Spain. The second landlord was much more pragmatic. After a short interview with us both and vetting our passports, he said he was happy to rent to us if I could provide bank and personal references from England, which I duly did, and two months' rent in advance, which, of course, Sam transferred over at once.

We moved into our new home on the 1st of December and it became one of the happiest times of my life since 2003, not just because we had four beds to choose from! With a real home and no financial worries, as Sam was helping us to pay the rent, given that neither of us was working, our relationship flourished. He was a kind, caring, loving partner and even had bouts of sheer romanticism. One evening, when I was feeling slightly down and homesick, he took me up to the roof and sat me down on one of the two kitchen chairs he had carried up. He then went back downstairs and returned with a jug of homemade sangria, two glasses and a couple of candles. We sat watching the stars and just talking until the early hours. He became even more imaginative on Valentine's Day when I made breakfast in bed—scrambled eggs and champagne (well cheap Cava really). He took the tray back to the kitchen and returned with a pot of chocolate mousse which he proceeded to spoon onto my breasts only to lick it off sucking my nipples, which he knew always turned me on. Since then, he has experimented with strawberry mousse and various flavours of ice cream (this only in hot weather).

However, during all this time, his English hasn't improved to any great extent. When he sets off with the shopping list, he usually has to check something. Broccoli is known as "That green stuff like trees". On the other hand, he certainly has no difficulty with clitoris, orgasm or 'shit I'm coming!' Thankfully for me. Who cares if the shopping is wrong! Christmas was really special with a lovely home and friends. I spent hours shopping, buying a tree and decorating the flat. I decorated every room and produced an amazing traditional Christmas lunch for five of us although it did make me feel a little homesick.

2007 was pretty uneventful. I travelled to the UK several times to see Sam, June and Helen, usually to babysit my beautiful granddaughter so that Sam and June could go away overnight for a couple of days. I always left a freezer full of food and a list of instructions for Paul. However, on one return from the UK, I found that the washing machine was broken. Paull had tried to wash seven pairs of jeans at once! False economy. It cost 90 euros to have it fixed!

At Easter of that year, I was lucky enough to travel with Sam, June and Helen to the Bahamas as resident grandma. I had been to the Bahamas on a family trip some years previously and never thought I would have the opportunity again. Naturally, the weather was perfect at that time of year and the hotel was excellent. The last time I visited the Bahamas, we stayed at the Ocean Club which was featured in one of Daniel Craig's Bond films. This time I was in the Atlantis which was equally luxurious. We spent most days by the pool and the evenings sampling the many different restaurants. But Sam has always had "itchy feet" and he and June decided to fly to Miami for a couple of days, leaving Helen and me to our own devices in the Bahamas. I must admit to being a little nervous at huge responsibility but we had a wonderful time on our own. I gave her first piece of bread during that time. Only a grandma could remember and be proud of that!

Paul and I loved living in the village and slowly but surely had become accepted as part of the community. The local church was the hub of the village along with Jose's bar in the small square. The priest could always be seen there after the service drinking with someone from the congregation! One Sunday after service, Paul decided that he would pay the reverend father's bill but as he was with two friends, and they had eaten which Paul didn't realise, it cost him 70 euros. Perhaps it was cheap for the absolution of our weekly sin of fornication. Paul couldn't take communion as he couldn't go to confession because he was "living over the brush" with me!

That summer, one of my sisters and her husband were travelling through Spain with a group of friends stopping off in Cuenca for two days. We arranged to meet them. It was the first time any of the family had met Paul. The meeting went well and we had a wonderful time. Strange as it may seem, Sam wasn't to meet Paul until our relationship was six years old! It was also that summer that I had to hurriedly return to England. I had a phone call in the early morning to say that Helen had been taken to hospital with suspected meningitis. I caught the first plane I could in the afternoon and went straight to the LGI. Fortunately, after several days, Helen made a full recovery.

In the spring of 2008, Sam had some financial issues so I tried to find a teaching job in the city. However, even with all my qualifications, I was told that I would need a TEFL certificate to teach outside the UK. I returned to Leeds and took and passed my TEFL course but still no luck. Now I was told that I had no experience! It was with a heavy heart that I had to make the decision to return to England as we couldn't afford to pay the rent without Sam's help. And so I left Murcia and Paul in September 2008.

Chapter 24
England Again!

It was with a mixture of complex emotions that I was, once again, leaving Spain and returning to England. I was sad, angry, frustrated, apprehensive and totally confused. Paul saw me off at the departure lounge, both of us fighting back the tears. He had already spent twenty minutes in the bathroom at home crying and I had cried almost all the way to the airport. For the umpteenth time in our relationship not knowing when we would see each other again, we said goodbye.

My flat in Rotherham felt cold, silent and lonely. Granted I still had family close by but they had their own lives and I always felt like an intruder, an unwelcome visitor. Fortunately, I made frequent visits to Leeds. I also had Emma, who turned out to be a true friend in a crisis even though she had so many of her own problems to deal with.

Paul stayed in the flat a few more weeks and then decided to move to Barcelona where he had friends. If my life was difficult, it was more so for him. But at least I had Helen's birthday to look forward to in early September and at Christmas, I was invited to Las Vegas for a week to spend the holidays with Sam, June and Helen... I wasn't looking forward to the flight on my own but the end result would be worth it, I kept telling myself. However, it wasn't as enjoyable as I had predicted. There was friction between Sam and June, and she flew back to England for Christmas. I was staying in a hotel as the rented apartment only had two bedrooms and at that time, a French au pair had been employed to look after Helen. Still it was a break from Rotherham. We had Christmas lunch at the Wynn Hotel and ate out most other days. I managed to speak to Paul once which made me feel rather sad having spent the two precious Christmases together so happily.

A new year almost always heralds change and so it was for me. But as always for me, it was for the worst and not for the better. Paul was having a terrible time in the squat in Spain. He had originally been staying in a friend's house but the friend had drunk and gambled his money away and the electricity had been cut off. There was no hot water, very little food and no loo paper! I sent emergency parcels when I could, rice, pasta, soups, toothpaste but it wasn't easy for me either.

I was being bombarded with letters from the solicitors who dealt with my divorce, stating that I owed money. I knew it couldn't be possible after three years and referred to the LCS. But the stress was unbearable. I was constantly at the doctors, the hospital, seeing a psychiatrist and having visits from a social worker, and drinking when I had money. By now, Mark had started to take the law into his own hands and begun to reduce the amount the court had awarded me.

It was at this point with everything whistling around in my head that I sat down, very calmly, and drank half a bottle of cheap white wine and very slowly started putting my prescribed drugs on the table in front of me. Even more slowly I began popping them into my mouth. And the phone rang...

Epilogue

Hindsight is a wonderful thing and if there is anything that I could change it would be to have stayed in my loveless marriage which would have meant that my mother and two siblings would not have had to suffer almost as much as I and become homeless in the bargain!

There is a period missing from these memories.

1978—July 1980, due to the fact that they concern the most important person in my life, in the past, now and until the time I leave this earth for hopefully a better place. A place where not only my sins will be truly forgiven but the person(s) who albeit temporarily, took away my sanity and changed the whole course of my life will receive divine retribution.

But if you want to find out please read *Still Alive*.